SPICE MAGIC

Published by Development Dynamics, Majon, 1a Furze
Lane, Purley, Surrey, CR8 3EJ

First published in Great Britain in 2001

ISBN 0 9536354 14

A catalogue record for this book is available from the
British Library.

Reprinted 2010

Printed by Vakil & Sons Pvt. Ltd.
Industry Manor, Appasaheb Marathe Marg, Worli,
Mumbai-400 025, India

Editor: Sara Goulden

Designer: Paul Webster

Photographer: Marcelo Saraiva

SPICE MAGIC

ACKNOWLEDGMENTS

I would like to thank:

My parents, Salim and Sherbanoo Nathani, whose warmth and hospitality are legendary. They had the good fortune to employ the best cook in Calcutta – Hassan – a legend in his own lifetime, who created the most delicious dishes for us, spoiling us forever.

My husband, Mehboob, and children, Kessy, Imraan and Rishad, for their support and encouragement in all my culinary forays – successes and disasters!

My sister, Junie, for her unwavering encouragement at every stage.

My brother, Mehmood, and my sister-in-law, Nina, for their abiding faith in my recipes.

Penny Wood, Steffi Barnes and Nicki Mcann, who share my passion for food.

My friends Françoise Smith and Ashraf Maladwala, who constantly reminded me about my commitment to produce this book, and Peter Cole, for being a willing guinea pig.

Carol Farley, Judy Grahame and Terry South, for their encouragement and enthusiasm.

Sara Goulden, my editor, not only for her thorough and diligent work, but also for her passionate involvement in and understanding of this project.

Finally, all those who have attended my seminars and cookery sessions and urged me to complete this adventure.

CONTENTS

Introduction **7**

The land where food is king **9**
The spice trail **13**
Spice of life **15**
Eating Indian-style **18**
Different regions, diverse dishes **20**
Popular dishes, enchanting myths **25**
Techniques **28**
Essential notes before you embark **30**
Starters **35**
Vegetables and vegetarian **51**
Meat **79**
Chicken **93**
Fish and seafood **107**
Rice **113**
Bread **127**
Accompaniments **133**
Desserts **139**

Appendix 1 Menu suggestions **147**
Appendix 2 If there is food, can drink be far behind? **148**
Appendix 3 Your food shall be your medicine **149**
Appendix 4 The Indian spice kitchen and the essential spice kitchen **152**
Appendix 5 Starters; Sweets and desserts; Utensils **156**
Hindi-English Glossary **158**
Bibliography **159**
Stockists **160**
Recipe index **162**
Recipe A-Z **166**

🦚 I N T R O D U C T I O N

AN INDIAN CULINARY ADVENTURE

Have you ever tasted a plate of chicken *tikka masala* perfumed with saffron, a mound of pilau rice peppered with cloves or a bowl of spicy Bombay potatoes sautéed with curry leaves and mustard seeds? If you don't know, then it's probable you haven't. You see, when a dish is cooked with the right spices, and in the right way, it will linger in the memory long after the meal is over. And once you have tasted such a dish, you will appreciate the magic that is infused into food with the addition of spices. They are the secret ingredients that can transform the ordinary into the extraordinary, the simple into the exotic and the mundane into the mouthwatering.

Since time immemorial, spices have added flavour and piquancy to what would otherwise be fairly bland preparations, and their enchantment has cast spells over rulers and their subjects alike. Once, they were the reason why explorers sailed the dangerous seas, countries were discovered and gold was traded. Today, of course, spices are easily available, yet they continue to fascinate all who cook with them, and there is no better place to start exploring their history and use than the food of India.

Spice Magic surveys the influence of history, culture, geography and religion on the food habits of India, which goes back hundreds of years in the development of its cuisine. A country with a rich cultural and historical fabric, India has assimilated the best of many age-old traditions and influences from various nations and religions while retaining two crucial elements: eating for good mental and physical health. Through this book you will discover the Indian spice kitchen, a clutch of unusual techniques and a number of regional variations, such as potatoes from Gujarat, *chana* (chickpeas) from Punjab and *bagara baigan* (spicy sautéed aubergine) from Hyderabad, with explanations about popular dishes and some of the enchanting legends behind them. Travelling to the heart of Indian cuisine, you will discover dishes created from simple recipes based on a group of key spices.

While some ingredients and spices in India may vary from region to region, a passion for food and recipes remains a constant throughout the land, and any Indian meal, with its tangy pickles, aromatic curries, flavoursome vegetables and satisfyingly sweet desserts, each one steeped in a subtle combination of spices, has the potential to become a magical feast. It will come as no surprise, then, that eating Indian-style can be a fascinating, intensely pleasurable experience – truly a feast for the senses.

THE LAND WHERE FOOD IS KING

India – the very word tends to conjure up images of the exotic, the mysterious and the magical. It is a country that, for hundreds of years, has captivated people with its splendid cultural heritage and its breathtaking natural beauty, yet it is only in the past few decades that its cuisine has captured the imaginations and appetites of people all over the world.

Yet I believe it is much misunderstood. Indians have always cooked using a huge range of spices, greater, perhaps, than in any other cuisine, and this has led many to categorise Indian food as 'hot'. While it is true that it is always tempered with a variety of herbs and spices, many Indian dishes, such as chicken korma and lamb *pasanda* (dishes cooked with rich spices), are not at all 'hot'. The heat is usually the result of the addition of chillies, which were only introduced into Asia in the 16th century by the Portuguese, who had discovered them in the New World. The history of Indian food dates back much further than that.

To understand the true art of Indian food and its unique place in world cuisine, it is important not only to be aware of spices, but of the manner in which Indian cooks use them. Each spice is prepared or used in a variety of ways in order to draw out different flavours – roasted, fried or ground, the result each time is quite distinctive.

The dish or pan in which the food is cooked also changes the character of its flavour. For example, meat cooked in a saucepan tastes quite different to meat cooked in a *tawa* (a slightly concave heavy-bottomed griddle pan made of cast iron), even if the ingredients used are identical, because each vessel conducts heat in a different way, altering the flavour of the final product, in the same way that chow mein cooked in an ordinary pan would taste different to chow mein cooked in a wok.

No journey to the heart of Indian cuisine would be complete without touching on the factors that have influenced its development. History, geography and religion have all played an important part, and an understanding of these is essential in order to truly appreciate the food of India.

History first: through the centuries India has been invaded by armies, traders and immigrants from all over the world. While some of India's conquerors are well-known – the Aryans, who invaded India from Persia at some point between 2000 BC and 1200 BC; the Moguls in the 16th century; and the British in the 18th and 19th centuries – there have been other invaders including the Arabs, Turks, Portuguese, French and Dutch. All played a part in influencing Indian culture, blending their own ways with those of the country they came to inhabit. Different groups introduced different spices; coriander and cumin seeds, for example, appeared on the Malabar Coast via the Mediterranean as a result of trade with the Arab world and Rome, while the East-facing coast adopted nutmeg and mace from China and the islands of Asia.

Though different parts of India demonstrate the presence of various communities, the Muslim invaders, the Moguls, in the northern part of India, made their mark most strongly, and indelibly etched their influence on Indian cuisine. As well as introducing brocades into India, the Moguls brought with them a taste for meat, certain drinks, spices and essences. Kormas and *pasandas* (dishes cooked with rich spices) are very much the *pièce de résistance* of Mogul food, whose range also includes biryanis (delicately flavoured rice with marinated meat) and rich desserts covered with nuts and edible silver leaf (*varq*). The Moguls also ushered in a sort of *haute cuisine* derived from the mild Persian preparations of pilaus (rice cooked with cloves, cinnamon sticks, cardamom pods and bay leaves and steamed using a special technique known as the *dum* technique) and kebabs (morsels of meat, marinated and grilled). Later, they incorporated the use of chillies and thereby produced an entirely new range of dishes. The Moguls' love of desserts led to the development of a repertoire of rich sweets made from sugar, milk and almonds, which has left most Indians with a very sweet tooth!

By the end of the 15th century, the lure of spices and the wealth and power that resulted from their trade gathered momentum. The French, English, Dutch, and Portuguese were all determined to join the race to establish their own power bases in India. With the arrival of these countries' representatives, an Indian influence on European cuisine emerged. As a result of the British Raj (the period of British rule in India), for example, Indian spices and delicacies were integrated with British dishes and ingredients to form a sort of Anglo-Indian cuisine (kedgeree, a dish of rice, fish and eggs, is an example of this hybridisation). Many British expatriates brought this cuisine back with them on their return to Britain, and their love of Indian food saw the gradual appearance of chutneys and curry powders on British shelves. Even after Independence, in 1947, the British fascination for the country known as the Jewel in the Crown continued, and it continues to this day, manifesting itself in the nation's enthusiasm for Indian food.

As to the other nations establishing themselves in India at the end of the 15th century, the Portuguese, who settled and remained in Goa, on the west coast of India, for many years, developed an interesting cuisine perhaps best known for the notoriously spicy vindaloo (a pork dish). While the French, based in southern India, developed a sort of Indian-Creole cuisine, including dishes such as *kari de boulettes* (lamb meatballs in tomato sauce) and *poulet rouge* (chicken with red spices). The spell had been cast.

While history played its role in the evolution of Indian cuisine, it was the geography of the country that determined, and to a certain extent still does, the availability of ingredients. Climate and soil conditions, which naturally dictate what may be cultivated in a particular region, have an inevitable impact on the diet of those who live there. In the north, for example, where wheat and millet is plentiful, people tend to eat more bread, whereas in the south and east rice is the staple, while the inhabitants of the coastal areas have developed a large range of dishes using coconut and fish.

It is only in recent years, with the introduction of more sophisticated transport and refrigeration, that fresh produce from different regions in India has started to appear in local markets there. Living in the West, we take it for granted that almost every vegetable will be available year-round on our supermarket shelves. However, the seasonal availability of certain vegetables is still very much in evidence in India where, even today, you have to wait for the right time of year to eat foods such as peas and mangoes. This, in my opinion, only adds to the pleasure of eating them.

Economic and social factors significantly affect what people can and cannot afford to eat in India. Kormas and *pasandas* may be popular Indian dishes in the West, but most people in India cannot afford the expensive ingredients, such as nuts, cream and saffron, that form an essential part of these rich preparations. The majority of Indians tend to eat simple, inexpensive food, consisting mainly of vegetables, lentils and rice. Meat and chicken are beyond the budget of a great many.

Though India has chosen to remain a secular country, the varied religious practices – many of them requiring strict adherence to specific dietary laws – of its inhabitants have been crucial in dictating what people will and will not eat. Of India's total population, 85 per cent are Hindus and 11 per cent are Muslims, with Jains, Sikhs, Christians, Zoroastrians and Buddhists making up the rest. While multicultural and multireligious societies are now fairly prevalent throughout the world, these groups have lived side-by-side in India for many centuries, contributing in no small measure to the varied texture of Indian life.

Hindus do not eat beef and Muslims do not eat pork, and in what could be interpreted as a gesture of goodwill of each religion towards the other pork and beef rarely figure prominently on restaurant menus or at dinner parties. Among the Hindus, certain communities practise vegetarianism.

The Jains, who strongly believe in the sanctity of life and oppose the ritual sacrifice of cattle, advocate strict vegetarianism – some are so strict they will not even eat root vegetables, such as onions and garlic, because roots have a potential for growth and eating them is considered tantamount to killing that potential. The presence of communities such as the Jains and the Buddhists, who also practise vegetarianism, has led to the growth of an interesting repertoire of solely vegetarian dishes, a fact often commented on by Westerners visiting India.

Inextricably linked with religion is the celebration of festivals, in which food plays a key role. Poverty in India is rampant, and while most people are preoccupied with the endless routine of earning what is considered in the West to be a meagre income (often not even enough to feed one person), a great amount of time and effort are invested in festivals – a welcome diversion from a difficult existence and the realities of a harsh life.

There are many festivals – some are of national importance, others are regional celebrations, others still are inspired by seasonal events, such as the harvest, but most have a religious significance. All of them provide an excuse for people to put on their best clothes, dressing in vivid colours and adorning themselves with flowers.

Among the Hindus, the most famous festival is Diwali, the Festival of Light, which marks the darkest night of the year, when dead souls are said to return to earth and must be shown the way by lights left on in houses. All over India, buildings, from ordinary houses to palaces, are illuminated, and fireworks are a typical element of the celebration. For most Hindus, especially businessmen, Diwali is the beginning of the Hindu new year, when everyone settles old debts and ancient feuds – a time for everyone to wish each other well. Two customs that have become an essential part of Diwali are the opening of new account books and the sending of sweets to neighbours, family, friends and business colleagues. The elaborate way in which these sweets and snacks are prepared at Diwali, as well as their sheer variety, is a highlight of the celebration. Not surprisingly, most sweetmeat sellers claim this to be their busiest and most lucrative period.

The largest minority religious group in India are the Muslims, and Eid is celebrated by them twice a year. The first is *Eid ul-Fitr*, which marks the end of Ramadan (a holy month of fasting), and the second is *Eid uz-Zoha*, which marks the end of the annual pilgrimage to Mecca (the *Hajj*). *Eid uz-Zoha* falls two months and 10 days after *Eid ul-Fitr*. Both Eids are festive occasions, when people buy new clothes, pray at the mosque, visit relatives and friends and feast on some of the most famous dishes in the Muslim repertoire, including biryanis (delicately flavoured rice with marinated meat), *murg mussalam* (chicken marinated and gently cooked with saffron and other exotic spices) and *seerkhurma* (a wonderfully rich milk drink).

THE SPICE TRAIL

As preservatives and flavourings for food, and as ingredients in cosmetics, fragrances and medicines, spices are known to have been used by man for 9,000 years. Warm, sweet, fragrant, pungent, fiery, exotic and mysterious, they have been the foundation of great fortunes, the causes of war and the subject of fascinating myths and legends.

Spices have captured imaginations through the centuries. An early example of a spice legend is the celebrated bible story of the meeting between the Queen of Sheba and King Solomon of Israel. Curious to know if reports of Solomon's wisdom and wealth were true, she travelled from Sheba to meet him, bringing with her camels bearing gifts of spices, such as saffron and cumin.

The spice trade has been in the hands of many different nations down the ages, among them the Phoenicians, Arabs, Venetians, Portuguese, Dutch and British. For about 2,000 years, from around 2000 BC, the Arabs dominated and controlled the spice trade, growing rich catering to the demands of the Romans, who were great lovers of spices. The Romans were determined to break the Arab monopoly, since so much of their own wealth was being used to pay for this expensive pleasure. This led to the Romans pursuing their own spice quest, undertaking dangerous voyages across the Indian Ocean for that purpose. The Romans introduced spices as varied as coriander seeds, caraway seeds, mustard seeds and cloves to Europe, but these were lost during the Dark Ages, only to be rediscovered during the Crusades.

The Roman spice 'habit' was fuelled by the requirements of a refined and creative cuisine. Apicius, a Roman gourmet of the first century, and supposed author of the oldest known cookbook in existence, *De re coquinaria* (On cooking), is said to have preferred to poison himself rather than lower his gastronomic standards. His recipes call for the use of spices that, at the time, would have been imported, including pepper, ginger, cardamom, nutmeg and asafoetida (a resinous plant gum with an ammoniac smell that becomes pleasantly garlicky on cooking).

The medieval period saw a great increase in Europe in the use of spices, which are said to have been used to disguise food that was past its best, pepper and ginger being the cheapest spices, used by all except the very poorest. Exotic spices bought by the wealthy were kept under lock and key and used only very sparingly. As people acquired a taste for them, the search for spices began in earnest. Though the quests were dangerous (involving long and perilous sea voyages), spices became a lucrative trade, and every European country harboured ambitions of dominating it. It was in this context that in 1497 Vasco da Gama arrived in India, declaring he had come for spices and Christians. The Dutch and British followed, setting up their own spice companies in India and thus changing the history of the country forever.

In the 17th century a slight setback in the use of spices occurred as a consequence of the Puritan belief that they 'inflamed passions'. As a result, the Puritans sought to have them banned. However their usefulness and versatility ensured they survived this temporary exile, and they have been used ever since, to the extent that in almost every corner of the globe life without them would be hard to imagine.

🌿 SPICE OF LIFE

Throughout history, the use of spices has been threefold – as preservatives, as seasonings and for medicinal purposes. Even in Roman times and the Middle Ages, herbs and spices were as much valued for their health-giving properties as for their flavour and it is uncommon to find a flavouring used solely for its taste. From comforting aches and pains to relieving toothaches, calming nerves, soothing colds, sweetening breath and giving skin a golden glow, the uses of spices are manifold.

The legends surrounding spices and the myths and folklore generated by them are both curious and intriguing, the most popular of all being the use of spices to create love potions and aphrodisiacs. Through the ages spices have also been used by husbands, wives and lovers to cast spells to prevent their partners from straying (red chillies), ensure their faithfulness (cumin seeds and dill), and arouse their passion (coriander seeds and dill). There is even a recipe, containing cloves, cardamom and cinnamon, for regaining the affections of an errant husband. In Britain, it was believed that an object containing caraway seeds would never be stolen, while in India, charred turmeric was used to keep evil spirits at bay (they were reputed to be repelled by the scent).

In India, the *Ayurveda* – Sanskrit writings in the ancient Hindu art of healing written some 3,000 years ago – attach special emphasis to the medicinal properties of spices. While only fairly recently in the West have we started to accept that what we eat determines in no small measure how healthy we are, this fact was already common knowledge in ancient India.

The *Ayurveda* notes that spices, while providing food with flavour, can also play a part in counteracting the effects of overindulgence, thus hot spices, such as pepper, chilli and ginger, are recommended to stimulate the appetite, while anise, dill and coriander seeds are prescribed to aid digestion. But the health-giving properties of spices, detailed in the *Ayurveda*, extend far beyond food. Chillies are recommended for the treatment of paralysis and digestive ailments; turmeric as a depilatory and to treat skin ailments; cardamom for halitosis, nausea, headaches, eye diseases and fever;

ginger as a remedy for liver complaints, flatulence and rheumatism; coriander for constipation, insomnia and childbearing; and cloves for fevers, dyspepsia, toning the heart, brain ailments, spleen, kidney, stomach and intestinal problems.

As well as describing the medicinal uses of spices, the *Ayurveda* discusses the subject of life in general and the importance of mental, as well as physical, health. That living well requires a good balance of mind, body and soul is a central theme of this treatise. Not surprisingly, therefore, the *Ayurveda* also describes methods of food preparation and consumption. According to the *Ayurveda*, it is important to prepare food in the right frame of mind – that is, with love and enthusiasm – and to eat in an atmosphere of tranquility. My own experience demonstrates this notion, as I know that when I cook with love and care, the dish definitely tastes better than when I have thrown the ingredients together in not the best of moods!

Interestingly, the *Ayurveda* does not prohibit the consumption of alcohol. The *Charaka Samhita* (the first and most important Ayurvedic text) lists 84 types of alcoholic preparation, attributing beneficial properties to them that include overcoming sleeplessness and grief, strengthening the mind and body, and aiding digestion.

There are almost as many myths and misconceptions about Indian cuisine as there are about the country itself, with many imagining the cuisine to involve large quantities of exotic spices, and thus to be extremely complicated, and not particularly healthy because of the 'heat' content of all the dishes. In fact, nothing could be further from the truth – Indian food can be made simply, using only a few core spices, and it can be both delicious and healthy when prepared in this manner. Though the word 'curry' seems to have become synonymous with spicy, mouth-burning Indian food, the range and repertoire of Indian cuisine is both much broader and more sophisticated than is generally assumed. In fact, the term 'curry' originates from the Tamil word *kari*, which means 'sauce', and a curry simply refers to a dish with a sauce (a 'wet' dish, as opposed to a dry one) and has nothing to do with strength or mildness of flavour.

The so-called curry powder popular outside India would never be used by any self-respecting Indian cook. Curry powder in the form sold in shops in the West gives food a harsh, acrid flavour, doing nothing to enhance the taste. Simple spices and herbs, properly combined, are what transform the appropriate raw ingredients into exotic Indian dishes. The good news is that as more and more people have come to realise this there has been an upsurge in the demand for Indian ingredients that are authentic and easily obtainable.

Masala is the Indian word for spices – the key to unlocking the door to the Alladin's cave of Indian cuisine. Though their flavour is the essence of their use, certain spices are used to please only the eye and to give the correct colour to a dish, as, for example, when freshly ground Kashmiri chillies are added to Goan fish curry to lend it its characteristic bright red hue.

The real art of Indian cookery lies in the blending of spices, and it is therefore important to know what is suited to a particular dish and its ingredients. Coriander seeds, turmeric and cumin are too strong and bitter for desserts, whereas cardamom and cinnamon are used in both savoury and sweet dishes. *Garam masala* – a blend of cardamom, cloves, cinnamon and bay leaves – is rarely used in vegetable or fish dishes, as the combined flavour of these potent spices overpowers more delicate flavours. Some spices are used more for their aroma than any other reason, especially in rice dishes such as pilaus and biryanis (delicately flavoured rice with marinated meat). Mustard seeds are indispensable in southern Indian cooking, in dishes such as *achaar gosht* (lamb with pickle spices), and when making pickles; and certain spices are used only during certain seasons – mace, for example, is not touched in the summer, as it is said to cause nosebleeds when consumed at that time of the year, whereas poppy seeds, which are reputed to have a cooling effect, are perfectly acceptable.

There are just a few rules as regards cooking with spices, the main one being that the spices should never taste raw and catch your throat. To avoid this, they should always be mellowed using a special frying technique called the *bhunao* technique, which I explain in detail on page 28.

In India, every cook has his or her own formula for a favourite dish, and agreement as to what constitutes a particular recipe is always open to discussion. Ultimately, every dish reflects the personality and taste of the cook, expressing his or her own unique style, and this is the beauty, and pleasure, of Indian cooking, whatever country or continent it is cooked in.

EATING INDIAN-STYLE

Any visitor to an Indian house will be struck immediately by the immense importance placed on hospitality and food. This can often reach embarrassing proportions, and the guest can sometimes find themself cajoled into having not just second but third and fourth helpings as well.

In India, any special occasion is seen as an excuse to invite people into the home, and, if this is not possible, it is customary to distribute food and sweets among family and friends. These occasions range from any of the numerous festivals to starting a new business venture, a wedding or success in an examination – all are good enough reasons to hold a feast. There is perhaps a religious significance to this preoccupation with food offerings: ancient Sanskrit scriptures state that 'annam Brahma' – 'food is God' – and add that, like God, food is what maintains all creatures.

AN INDIAN MEAL

Many people wonder how Indians can survive on a diet of rich, spicy food, but this is only because they assume Indians eat vindaloo (one of the spiciest curries in the repertoire of Indian food) and chicken *tikka masala* (marinated smoked chicken in a rich, creamy sauce) on a daily basis, with the occasional onion *bhajiya* (deep-fried onion fritter) thrown in for good measure! Nothing could be further from the truth – as I have already explained, most Indian meals are simple and highly nutritious.

A typical Indian meal combines carbohydrate, protein and vegetables. When I was growing up in Calcutta, the main daily meal would consist of a vegetable dish, chapatis (flat bread), a meat, chicken or fish curry, rice, raita and *cachumbar* (raw vegetable relish). Desserts were for special occasions only.

There are no starters and main courses, as such, and all the dishes are served simultaneously. While *thalis* (large steel platters) and banana leaves are still frequently used (the latter mainly at rural weddings and large gatherings, to eliminate the need to wash dishes), normal china is the rule in most houses in the larger cities. *Katoris* (small steel bowls) are often used to separate the different dishes, and are particularly useful for dishes with runny sauces, such as *dahi ki curry* (yogurt curry) or *daal gosht* (spicy lentils with lamb). A meal in a typical middle-class Indian home usually consists of one or two vegetable dishes, chapatis, *puris* or *parathas* (different types of bread), a meat, chicken or fish curry (or a lentil dish – daal, or yogurt curry for vegetarians), rice, pickles (*achaars*), raita and sometimes cutlets or kebabs (dishes that would be classed as starters in the West).

Indian desserts are far more interesting and varied than the limited items that appear in Indian restaurants in the West, and they are not always as rich as they are often portrayed. The Bengali dessert *mishti doi* (a sweet caramelized yogurt) is not only incredibly delicious but, as it is not excessively sweet, nor is it full of ghee (clarified butter), butter or cream, it is (at least by Indian standards!) fairly healthy. *Sandesh* (another Bengali speciality, which can be bought in the many sweetmeat shops that line the streets of Calcutta), is a cottage-cheese and sugar-based fudge flavoured with lemon, orange, saffron or chocolate; another example of a healthier dessert (again, it doesn't contain ghee, butter or cream).

At the end of an Indian meal, *paan* is often served. *Paan* serves as an aid to digestion and also acts as an astringent to remove and neutralise the taste of food in the mouth. It consists of a *paan* or betel leaf filled with dozens of ingredients, ranging from cardamom, cloves and aniseed to betel nuts. *Paans* can be simple or elaborate, and, years ago, the serving of *paan* prepared at home was an elegant experience. The *paan-daan*, with its delicate designs and filigreed silver containers, was brought out after a meal and normally grandmothers had the honour of painstakingly preparing the *paan* using their own special ingredients. (Please note: Betel-nut and *paan* chewing are factors directly associated with oral cancer. For more information, contact the British Dental Association or the American Dental Association.)

Most Indian people eat with their fingers. Though this may appear to be rather a messy habit, eating nimbly with your fingers, once you get used to it, is quite an art form and one that, for some inexplicable reason, makes certain foods taste better. There is a story that on a visit to India the Shah of Iran experimented eating Indian-style with his fingers. He was reported to be so charmed he decided that eating Indian food with a knife and fork was like making love through an interpreter!

DIFFERENT REGIONS, DIVERSE DISHES

NORTHERN INDIA

Northern India is home to what is probably the most famous style of Indian cuisine – Mogul cuisine. More than any other example of Indian cooking, Mogul recipes constitute the main body of those that have become Indian classics in the West, the most popular dishes being kormas and *pasandas* (dishes cooked with rich spices) and biryanis (delicately flavoured rice with marinated meat).

Kashmir Often referred to as the Switzerland of the East, Kashmir, in the far north of India, is a land of spectacular natural beauty made up of mountains and lakes. Inhabited by both Hindus and Muslims, many of the Hindus in Kashmir are Brahmins (the high priestly class to which the powerful Nehru family belonged). While most Brahmins elsewhere in India abhor meat, the Kashmiri Brahmins eat it with relish, though they refrain from eating garlic and onions, which they feel encourage base passions. Kashmiri Muslims share many common dishes with their Hindu counterparts, but use liberal quantities of onions and garlic.

Best-known dishes: rogan josh (spicy red lamb cooked with yogurt and saffron); *kofta* curry (*koftas* are similar to meatballs)

Punjab Punjab, in the northern part of India, known as the land of the five rivers and as the granary of India, has been greatly influenced by various invaders, among them Alexander the Great, Nadir Shah (Persia), Babar (Mongolia) and Sher Shah (Afghanistan). Punjab is the home of the famous *tandoor* (traditional clay oven) – the secret ingredient in Punjabi cooking. *Tandoors* started out as social institutions as much as a means of cooking – they were difficult to set up in individual homes and so communal *tandoors* were used by people to cook meats and breads prepared at home, offering the opportunity to meet people and exchange news and gossip at the same time.

Punjab is also famous for its *dhabas* – roadside cafés, patronised originally by the thousands of truck drivers who travelled the network of motorways in the area. The concept thrived and spread, and *dhabas* became fashionable among students for providing tasty, good-value meals. They then became an integral part of the food scene of northern India.

Best-known dishes: tandoori chicken; *kaali* daal (a dish made with whole black lentils); naan bread; stuffed *parathas* (flat bread)

Lucknow   In the 18th century, in what was once known as the state of Avadh (now Lucknow), a style of cooking flourished that was to become a classic technique – *dumpukht*. And in India today, the *dumpukht* (*dum*) style is staging a comeback.

Dum involves cooking the dish in its own steam, and is a style that originated in Persia, where the prepared dish was sealed and buried in the hot sands of the desert to bring forth the best flavours. Biryani is probably the best modern example of a dish cooked using this technique.

In India, *dum* became a popular method of cooking during the hard times of the mid 18th century, when nawab (prince) Asaf ud Daulah decided to provide jobs for his subjects by commissioning a monument that was to be built during the day and destroyed at night, thus ensuring they had continuous employment. During this operation, large quantities of food were cooked, then sealed in pans called *degchis* and kept warm in large double-walled ovens. The gentle steaming that resulted added a deliciously subtle flavour to the food. One day, the nawab sampled a dish cooked in this way and was so impressed he adapted it for royal banquets and hunts.

During this period, the nawab's chefs would vie with each other to produce exotic, aromatic dishes with aphrodisiac qualities, enhanced with unusual herbs and spices, to further boost their reputations and curry (!) favour with the nawab.

Best-known dishes: murg mussalam (chicken marinated and gently cooked with saffron and other exotic spices); nahari (aromatic dish of lamb cooked in yogurt and spices); korma and *pasanda* (dishes cooked with rich spices); biryani (delicately flavoured rice with marinated meat)

Rajasthan   A state in northern India bordering Pakistan, Rajasthan is the home of the Thar Desert, where conditions are arid and the terrain difficult. Once known as the land of princes (*maharajas*), this area is now famous for having the shrewdest business community in India. The *maharajas* were passionate about hunting, and as a result they developed a love for game. Pheasant, peacock, quail and duck, as well as wild boar and venison, can all be found in the desert, and exotic dishes incorporating them were created to satisfy the sophisticated palates of the *maharajas*. Game cooking is a highly respected art form, requiring skills that are hard to master, and game meat at the time of the *maharajas* was highly prized, and was often pickled and preserved. A particular delicacy was rind of boar, which was often kept under lock and key and was only to be offered to honoured guests!

In contrast to game cooking, the region is also famous for the simple, flavourful vegetarian cooking of the Maheshwaris, a community from Marwar (a part of Rajasthan). This encompasses dishes made primarily from lentils (daal) and vegetables, with the liberal use of asafoetida (an ingredient rarely used in Western cooking, but prevalent throughout India), which tastes a bit like garlic when cooked, and *amchoor* (mango powder). Tomatoes do not feature in any of the recipes, as they do not grow in this region, and in the past onions and garlic were never used, as it was feared they would excite passions!

Best-known dishes: sule (a smoked Rajasthani kebab that can be barbecued in 11 different ways); *moong daal khilma* (a dry dish made with moong daal and tempered with asafoetida, cumin seeds and other spices)

THE WESTERN COAST

Goa   Goa offers an incredible cuisine influenced by the Christians, Hindus, Muslims and Portuguese who have all played a part in its history and culture. A rich variety of culinary styles have emerged from this small area, which was colonised by the Portuguese for many years. Goan food is generally chilli hot and features coconut and vinegar.

Best-known dishes: vindaloo (a very spicy pork dish); spicy Goan prawns

Kutch   Kutch lies on the northwest coast of India, bordered on one side by sea and on the other by desert. For a long time, its only means of communication for overseas trade, and even with the rest of India, was by sea. Its insular location and arid desert soil is said to have produced a resilient and hardy people.

Kutch is home to the Khojas, among others, a community that converted to Islam from Hinduism some 500 years ago. Khojas, though mainly employed in business, are famous for producing professional men in many walks of life. For example, Jinnah, the founder of Pakistan, was a Khoja.

Today, Khojas live all over the world – East Africa, Madagascar, Pakistan, the Persian Gulf, the USA, Canada and Australia – and Khoja cuisine has been influenced enormously by the movement of its people to other parts of the world. The move to East Africa saw the emergence of dishes that resulted from the use of different indigenous ingredients. In India, the cooks employed by Khojas often came from the state of Uttar Pradesh in northern India, leading to a Mogul influence on many Khoja dishes.

Best-known dishes: khichra (a dish made with wheat, lentils, meat and spices); *samosas* (triangular parcels of very thin pastry stuffed with lamb, chicken or vegetables); biryani (delicately flavoured rice with marinated meat)

Gujarat 'If the diet is pure, the mind will be pure, and if the mind is pure, the intellect will be pure,' wrote Manu, the great Hindu lawgiver. Purity of mind and spirit is a cardinal Hindu virtue, ranking in importance alongside self-control, detachment and non-violence. For many millions of Indians, purity of the mind and spirit demands a diet of such strict vegetarianism that not only meat, fish and poultry, but even eggs are forbidden. To some Hindus, even blood-coloured vegetables, such as beetroot and tomatoes, are unacceptable. Others refuse to eat root vegetables, such as carrots and potatoes, because the process of pulling them from the ground might cause the death of earthworms or grubs, and even this indirect way of taking life is considered sinful. One result of this deeply held tradition of vegetarianism is that India has produced one of the most varied and imaginative vegetarian cuisines in the world.

India's vegetarianism comes essentially from the Hindu sects, but also from Jains, many of whom are Gujaratis, and if there is an *haute cuisine* for vegetarians, then it can be found in the state of Gujarat. Delicate *khandvi* (a savoury rolled crepe made with gram flour and yogurt) and spongy *doklas* (savoury lentil, flour or rice cakes) are specialities.

Gujaratis are renowned for the simplicity of their lifestyle, and this lack of fussiness is reflected in their cuisine. Traditionally, Gujaratis eat from *thalis*, steel platters holding several *katoris* (little bowls), each one filled with a small quantity of a different dish.

Gujaratis are also known for a variety of snacks, which have become popular all over India. Most famous among these are *bhel puri* (puffed rice, lentils, chopped onions, herbs and two types of chutney) and *pani puri* (little fried pastry bits seasoned with spices).

Best-known dishes: doklas; khandvi; srikhand (a saffron-flavoured yogurt dessert)

Parsees In the incredibly varied patterns that make up life in India, some small ethnic communities exist, which, though undeniably Indian, have evolved their own distinctive habits and customs. These include the Syrian Christians, Jains and Parsees. The Parsees fled from Persia over 1,000 years ago to escape religious persecution, and eventually settled in the state of Gujarat and the city of Bombay. They have retained a great deal of their ancient heritage in their religious and food habits. Although most Parsees adhere strictly to Zoroastrianism, they are one of the most Westernised of all Indian communities. They have no food restrictions, though some do not eat beef in deference to a promise made when they sought asylum in a Hindu kingdom in western India over a thousand years ago. Their food is a delicious blend of sweet and sour flavours, brilliantly spiced with the more traditional Indian spices, such as coriander and cumin seeds.

Best-known dishes: dhansak (a robust dish containing meat, puréed lentils, vegetables and spices); *patia* (a sweet and sour dish); *patarani machi* (fish wrapped in a banana leaf and steamed)

SOUTHERN INDIA (including Hyderabad)

There is a prevailing misconception that southern Indian food is primarily vegetarian. Although southern India did remain relatively untouched by the Muslim invasion, its cuisine includes a range of wonderful non-vegetarian dishes, particularly seafood dishes.

The most notable feature of southern Indian cooking is a liberal use of coconut, curry leaves, tamarind and fenugreek seeds. Most southern food is not hot, except for the cuisine of the states of Andhra Pradesh and Kerala.

Many superb culinary styles have evolved in southern India – Malabari, Coorgi (Coorg is a district of Karnataka), Syrian Christian and Hyderabadi Muslim. Hyderabadi cuisine evolved in the wealthy Muslim court that held sway in the heart of Hindu India in the 18th century. While it combines the best of the Muslim tradition – kebabs, kormas (dishes cooked with rich spices) and yogurt dishes – it also includes the unique flavours of the south: curry leaves, chillies and mustard seeds.

Best-known dishes: dosas (large crepes made with a rice-flour batter); *idlis* (large steamed rice-flour dumplings); *upma* (semolina tempered with mustard seeds and curry leaves); *aviyal* (vegetable curry cooked with coconut and yogurt); Hyderabadi biryani (biryani – delicately flavoured rice with marinated meat – with the addition of nuts)

POPULAR DISHES, ENCHANTING MYTHS

There is an ongoing debate as to what defines authentic Indian dishes, because for hundreds of years the secrets of the treasure trove of Indian recipes remained jealously guarded. Professional cooks, who worked for royalty and some of the wealthier families, were reluctant to impart their trade secrets for fear of losing their power and being surpassed by others. Even when we questioned our own family cook about the ingredients in a dish, he was always evasive and gave as few details as he could get away with. Finally, however, he decided I could be entrusted with some of his techniques, and after I had married and settled in England he painstakingly showed me how to cook many dishes on my trips back to Calcutta. Needless to say, these have helped me enormously, and without the benefit of his know-how this book would never have come to fruition.

An important aspect of Indian food is that there is no collection of dishes that one could categorise as *the* national cuisine, because regional variations and distinctive food habits have produced a plethora of widely differing dishes. In the West at one time, all Indian food was referred to as curry, even though a curry in India merely refers to a dish with a lot of sauce.

Though there are as many versions of popular Indian dishes as there are cooks, some aspects of a dish will remain central to its character, and while every restaurant and Indian food enthusiast will claim their version to be the real thing, it is interesting to note that there have been known to be up to five different interpretations of the same dish within one square mile of Indian restaurants! Here I have listed the most popular dishes and some of the legends behind them.

Biryani   One of many dishes of Mogul origin, lamb biryani is the most popular version of this rice dish. Here, the rice is cooked separately and arranged on top of the cooked meat, which has been marinated in browned onions, yogurt and whole *garam masala* (cloves, bay leaves, cinnamon sticks and cardamom pods). The rice is then sprinkled with saffron-infused milk and the entire dish is tightly sealed and cooked very slowly in the oven (the *dum* technique). The end result is an intensely aromatic dish. Biryanis are never served with a vegetable curry, as is often the case in Indian restaurants in the West, as this detracts from the subtle flavours. They are usually accompanied by a raita or *cachumbar* (raw vegetable relish).

Dhansak A popular Parsee speciality, this combines a variety of lentils (daals) – sometimes up to six types are used – with lamb and vegetables, including aubergine, pumpkin, marrow, potatoes and tomatoes, and is traditionally served with brown rice.

Do Pyaza *Do* means 'two' and *pyaz* means 'onions', and this dish consists of meat cooked in ghee (clarified butter) with double the quantity of onions. The story goes that a certain mullah (learned Muslim), who was one of the nine 'jewels' in the court of Akbar the Great (Mogul emperor of India in the last half of the 16th century), was also a gourmet and a gourmand, and this dish is an example of the mullah's culinary ingenuity. The mullah kept an open house, and a steady stream of guests would arrive all evening, often many more than were expected. At some point the mullah would realize the food would not be sufficient for all those who had stopped by. He would then clap his hands, indicating to the kitchen that more onions should be added to the meat to make it go further, and in this way he realized that adding twice the quantity of onions to meat made the original dish taste even better.

Jalfrezi This was originally made with leftover meat. *Jhal* means 'spicy', and it was the presence of fresh red chillies, which were fried with the meat along with potatoes, that gave this dish its fiery taste. Today, variations include serving it with thinly sliced onions, peppers and tomatoes. Vegetable *jalfrezi* is a popular vegetarian alternative.

Korma This is a rich dish of Mogul origin. The Mogul era was unrivalled in the showiness of its hospitality and its concern for style and luxury, and its cuisine is one of the many legacies bequeathed to India by rulers known for their extravagance and delight in material comfort. Kormas are either white or red in colour; and both include yogurt in their ingredients. White korma – or *safed korma*, as it is known – contains almonds, cream and coconut, and is milder and more easily appreciated by newcomers to the world of Indian food than the spicier red version.

Patia This is a sweet and sour dish with its roots in the Parsee community. After arriving in India over 1,000 years ago having fled Persia, the Parsees had to persuade the ruler to let them stay. It is said that the ruler at the time insisted there was no room for them in his land, and to illustrate the point he filled a large bowl with milk until it was so full not one more drop could be added without it overflowing. The Parsee leader then took some sugar and carefully added it to the milk. He waited until it had dissolved, then turned to the bemused ruler and said that this proved the Parsee community would sweeten the country without displacing anyone!

Patia contains tamarind, which provides the sour taste, and jaggery (*gur*), a coarse brown sugar similar to molasses, which provides the sweetness. Prawn *patia* is the most popular version of this dish.

Pilau   To make basic pilau rice, plain rice (preferably basmati) is sautéed in oil, ghee (clarified butter) or butter with whole *garam masala* (cloves, bay leaves, cinnamon sticks and cardamom pods), and it is then cooked in a precise quantity of water. Originally, rice cooked in meat stock was known as pilau, but today, any rice preparation that is not merely boiled and drained is referred to as pilau rice.

Tandoori dishes   The *tandoor* is a traditional clay oven fired by charcoal, which, when heated, releases a unique mellow fragrance that permeates food. Efforts to duplicate the flavour without the use of a *tandoor* have proved difficult. The charcoal fire on the flat bottom of the *tandoor* heats the sides to scorching point to about half-way up, and to a hot glow for the top half. To achieve this distribution, the *tandoor* must be lit at least a couple of hours before anything is cooked in it. Tradition holds that a *tandoor* will improve the flavour of anything cooked in it, though this depends on the *tandoor*. With tandoori meat dishes, the time spent marinating the meat is crucial, as is the basting, since this seals the flavour and makes the meat succulent. Tandoori chicken and tandoori naan are two of the most popular examples of this type of cooking.

Vindaloo   A contribution from the Konkani-speaking Christians of western India, this very spicy pork dish has a semi-Portuguese name, and the 'vin' in *vindaloo* indicates that the meat is cooked in either wine or vinegar, which is added to both tenderize and preserve it. It generally tastes better when it is one-day old and takes on a pickled effect. It is very popular in Goa.

✿ TECHNIQUES

While fresh herbs and spices are essential for making a successful meal, the key to Indian cooking lies in the understanding and practice of four fundamental techniques. Simple and easy to master, they will ensure mouthwatering results every time.

Bhunao This is the process of cooking spices at a high temperature and adding tablespoons of water, stock or yogurt to lower the temperature and prolong the time the spices can be cooked without burning and drying out.

The reasoning behind this technique is to allow the spices to blend together so as not to taste raw or catch the throat. This technique is the key to Mogul cooking, and it requires patience and practice. As you *bhunao*, you will notice the oil start to separate from the spices: this is the sign that the spices have blended properly. Many of the recipes in this book use this technique, but two particularly good examples are *gosht-e-Mehboob* (tender pieces of lamb in a rich, robust sauce) and *murgi ka salna* (simple, everyday chicken curry).

Dhuan This is the technique of imparting a smoky flavour to a dish, and is particularly useful when there is no access to a barbecue or *tandoor* (traditional clay oven). A piece of coal is heated until it is red-hot and then placed in the middle of the ingredients to be smoked (which must be placed in a heatproof dish). Oil is immediately poured over the coal, which releases smoke, at which point the dish is covered tightly, either with kitchen foil or a lid, and set aside to allow the smoke to permeate the food. After a short time (15-45 minutes, depending on how much time you have), the dish can be cooked as required, though the coal should obviously be discarded before cooking! This technique is most often used for chicken or smoked salmon *tikkas*, and kebabs, but it also imparts a wonderful flavour to certain curry dishes, such as *kuku paka* (chicken with a sauce of creamy coconut, fresh coriander and lemon juice).

Dum   This is the process of cooking a dish in its own steam, and is most commonly used for rice dishes, such as pilaus and biryanis (delicately flavoured rice with marinated meat). After certain initial preparations, the required ingredients are placed in a pot or pan, which is tightly sealed and left to cook at a very low temperature (usually in the oven) so as to allow the flavours to blend. Before sealing, a small amount of liquid is added to the ingredients to provide the steam that will complete the cooking. When the dish is unsealed, the most wonderful aromas are released.

When ovens were not used, hot coals were usually placed on top of the sealed pot so as to provide a balanced heat. Cooking using the *dum* technique produces incredibly subtle, fragrant results, and while it is an old technique, it has become very popular among contemporary Indian chefs, who have been known to devote entire menus to dishes cooked in this way. Dishes using this technique include *masoor* pilau (rice with mince and lentils).

Tarka or bagaar   Adding certain ingredients (usually spices) to very hot oil in order to release their flavour is called *tarka* or *bagaar*, and this process can be performed at the beginning or end of the cooking process. The oil is heated until it is very hot and the required ingredients are dropped in, releasing their flavour as they hit the oil. If *tarka* or *bagaar* is taking place at the start of the cooking process, the remaining ingredients are then added to the oil and cooked according to the recipe; if *tarka* or *bagaar* is taking place at the end of cooking, the infused oil is poured over the prepared ingredients, which are then covered for a few moments to allow the full flavour to be infused. The ingredients that respond most successfully to this technique include cumin seeds, mustard seeds, garlic, onions, chilli powder, cloves and curry leaves.

The temperature of the oil is crucial. If the oil gets too hot, the spices will burn; yet if it is not hot enough the flavour of the spices will not be released. In order to ensure the oil is hot enough, drop in a tiny quantity of the ingredient being used (eg a single curry leaf or a couple of mustard seeds) to test it first – if the ingredient turns a darker shade, sizzles and splutters, the oil is ready. If the ingredient turns very dark, reduce the heat and add the remainder after 1 minute. Dishes using this technique include *masala wale aloo* (spicy Bombay potatoes), *tarka* daal (lentils infused with garlic) and quick green beans.

ESSENTIAL NOTES BEFORE YOU EMBARK

Chicken Though most people prefer boneless chicken, chicken dishes prepared with chicken on the bone tend to have a better flavour. Either can be used for the recipes in this book. The skin should always be removed.

Coriander-cumin powder Where I have mentioned coriander-cumin powder in this book, I refer to a powder called *dhania-jeera* in India, which is simply a combination of coriander powder and cumin powder. If you use both powders separately and in the correct proportions (ie half each of the full amount of coriander-cumin powder), the end result will be the same.

Daal This refers to any member of the legume or pulse family (usually lentils), the most popular types being *chana* (golden yellow lentils), *moong* (split mung beans), *masoor* (red lentils) and *toor* (deep yellow lentils).

Flour (gram and atta) Two types of flour are used in this book that are not commonly found on the shelves of supermarkets in the West. Gram flour (*besan*) is flour made from *chana* daal (golden yellow lentils) and *atta* is a wholemeal flour. Wholemeal and plain flour combined in equal quantity can be substituted for *atta*.

Freezing Indian food Most Indian dishes freeze very well, apart from dishes incorporating potatoes. If these are required for a dish that is being frozen, they should be freshly cooked just before serving.

Fresh coriander leaves There is no substitute for fresh coriander leaves – I believe you can never use too many of them. The best way to store the leaves is to put the stalks in a jar of cold water and keep it in the fridge; they will last much longer this way. If you have bought a very large quantity, chop it all and keep it in an airtight container in the freezer, adding however much you need to the dish during cooking (as opposed to scattering it over the cooked dish just before serving). However, be warned – frozen coriander leaves do not have the same flavour as fresh.

Garam masala *Garam masala* literally means 'hot spices'. It is a mixture of several different spices, and many people make their own powder at home with different combinations, sometimes including spices such as mace, peppercorns and nutmeg. In its powdered form it should be used very sparingly and only at the end of preparing a dish, usually as a garnish. *Garam masala* spices used whole (eg whole cloves, bay leaves, cinnamon sticks and cardamom pods) add a wonderful warmth and richness to food and can be added from the beginning of cooking. The less edible elements of whole *garam masala*, such as cinnamon sticks, can be fished out by the cook at the end of cooking, though in India they are usually left in and discreetly removed by each diner to the side of their plate should they happen to find any in their portion.

Getting the portions right All the recipes in this book will serve four people as part of a typical Indian meal, which is composed of bread (such as naan), rice (such as pilau), raita or *cachumbar* (raw vegetable relish), a meat, fish or vegetable curry and one vegetable dish (a starter is optional). If making only one main dish, the quantity will be sufficient for two people only. Water can be added to sauces if a thinner consistency is preferred. Special rice dishes, such as biryanis (delicately flavoured rice with marinated meat), don't require an additional curry, and should simply be accompanied by a raita or *cachumbar* (raw vegetable relish).

Hara masala This wonderfully vibrant paste, made from fresh coriander and green chillies, is a staple of Indian cooking, and one that I use in many of the recipes in this book.
To make 5 tablespoons of hara masala: Take 125g (4½oz) of chopped fresh coriander leaves, 2 green chillies and 1 tablespoon of lemon juice. Put the coriander leaves and green chillies into a food processor, or a pestle and mortar, add 4-5 tablespoons of water and blend, or crush, until you have a fine paste. Stir in the lemon juice and refrigerate. This will keep in the fridge for up to 7 days. You can also freeze individual portions in an ice-cube tray, using them as and when you need them. This can be frozen for up to 2 months.

Marinating The longer you can leave a piece of meat, chicken or fish to marinate, the better – with chicken *tikkas* I sometimes even leave them overnight. I recommend marinating for at least an hour; if that's not possible, then as long as you can!

Oil Corn oil is my favourite, and the oil I would recommend for all the recipes in this book. When using the *bhunao* technique (see page 28), it is advisable to be generous with the oil, as this helps to amalgamate the spices. If there is too much extra oil floating on the surface of the dish once it is cooked, it can be easily removed with a spoon. Alternatively, the curry can be refrigerated, allowing the oil to solidify on top and then be removed. Traditionally, ghee (clarified butter) is used in India, instead of oil. It definitely gives a better flavour and is said to have a cooling effect on the body; it is also supposed to be very good at bringing out the best flavours of the ingredients cooked in it. However, it is now out of favour due to its high cholesterol content. Butter is not recommended, since most curries require the onions and spices to be fried for quite a while, and butter burns easily.

Onions You can use either red or white onions for any of the recipes requiring them in this book, though I do find red onions add a particularly good flavour, not only to the red curries, such as *rogan josh* (spicy red lamb cooked with yogurt and saffron), *gosht-e-Mehboob* (tender pieces of lamb in a rich, robust sauce) and *murgi ka salna* (simple, everyday chicken curry), but also to biryanis (delicately flavoured rice with marinated meat). It is important to chop the onions to a uniform size and to brown them to the shade required by the recipe. Browning onions is a time-consuming task, but is crucial to the taste and appearance of a curry.

Pressure cooking If you feel comfortable using a pressure cooker, you can save yourself a great deal of time in the kitchen. A pressure cooker is especially helpful for cooking meat and lentils, both of which take only 15 minutes to cook in one. If you do use a pressure cooker, proceed with caution.

Puréed ginger and puréed garlic Almost all the savoury recipes in this book call for these two ingredients, and it is as important to make sure they are puréed as it is to use fresh spices. However, puréeing small quantities of ginger and garlic can be time-consuming, so here I have included chilling and freezing instructions in the methods for each. In many homes in India a person will be employed whose job, among other things, involves preparing certain ingredients at the beginning of each day, so that they are ready for the day's cooking. These normally include puréeing the ginger and garlic, as well as chopping the chillies, fresh coriander leaves and fresh mint.

To make 8 tablespoons of puréed ginger: Take 200g (7oz) of fresh ginger. Peel, wash and cut it into pieces. Place the pieces in a food processor, or in a mortar and pestle, with 4 tablespoons of water and blend, or crush, until you have a smooth paste. Stir in 1 teaspoon of oil, to help preserve the paste, and refrigerate. This will keep in the fridge for up to 7 days. You can also freeze individual portions in an ice-cube tray, using them as and when you need them. This can be frozen for up to 2 months.

To make 8 tablespoons of puréed garlic: Take 200g (7oz) of garlic cloves. Peel the cloves, place them in a food processor, or in a mortar and pestle, with 4 tablespoons of water and blend, or crush, until you have a fine paste. Stir in 1 teaspoon of oil, to help preserve the paste, and refrigerate. This will keep in the fridge for up to 7 days. You can also freeze individual portions in an ice-cube tray, using them as and when you need them. This can be frozen for up to 2 months.

Rice   Rice should be stored in a cool place and should always be soaked for 30 minutes before using, then rinsed out several times under cold running water in order to remove the starch, which is what makes it sticky.

Salt   Salt brings out the flavour of Indian food, so please, if you can, be more generous than you would normally be – it can make all the difference between a tasty curry and a tasteless one. For every recipe requiring salt in this book, a minimum of a quarter of a level teaspoon is required, but you will probably find you need anything from half a level teaspoon up to two.

Spices – whole versus ready-ground   It seems obvious, but, if possible, it is always better to grind spices from whole as and when you need them rather than buy them ready-ground, because even if stored in airtight containers most spices lose their aroma and flavour very quickly. If grinding spices every time you want to use them is inconvenient and you prefer to buy ready-ground, they should be bought in small quantities and used as soon as possible after purchasing. Certain spices, however, including chilli powder, tend to hold on to their qualities even if stored for a longer period of time.

Spiciness   Most of the recipes in this book, apart from chicken Madras and *masala wale aloo* (spicy Bombay potatoes) – both very spicy – are medium hot. However, the spice content can be adjusted according to taste – it is entirely up to you.

Spoonfuls   All spoonfuls are level.

Storing spices   Spices should always be kept in cool, dark places, and not exposed to sunlight or heat, which would lead to a rapid loss of flavour.

Using the right pan   The utensil in which you cook your food will affect the character of the end result because of the way in which heat is transmitted. Where I have suggested a particular pan, do try to get hold of it if you don't already have one. For the *bhunao* technique (see page 28), it is important to fry the spices over a high heat, and thick copper-bottomed pots or *handis* are ideal for this.

Note to US readers   250ml = 1 cup

❧ S T A R T E R S

Sizzling hot bhajiyas; mouthwatering kebabs; spicy potato patties; fragrant smoked salmon tikkas... A myriad wonderful ways to begin a memorable feast, or a great canapé menu for a drinks party.

ASSORTED BHAJIYAS
Deep-fried vegetable fritters

Bhajiyas are popular mid-afternoon snacks, usually served with a range of chutneys. Vegetables are the most popular ingredients used for making them, though prawns (shrimps) and small pieces of chicken also work well. They are best cooked in a *karai* or wok-like pan, as the shape makes it easier to deep-fry them. The range of chutneys with which to eat *bhajiyas* includes *mitha* (tamarind and date), *hara* (fresh coriander) and *pudina* (mint). You will find recipes for these later on in this book; or you could just serve the *bhajiyas* with good old tomato ketchup! The vegetables should be sliced thinly enough for it to take only a couple of minutes to deep-fry each piece.

225g (8oz) gram flour (besan; see Stockists)
pinch turmeric
pinch chilli powder
15g (½oz) finely chopped fresh coriander leaves
¼ teaspoon baking powder or bicarbonate of soda
oil, for deep-frying
2 medium potatoes, peeled and thinly sliced
2 green peppers, deseeded and chopped into 5cm (2in) squares
1 small aubergine (eggplant), thinly sliced
1 courgette (zucchini), sliced into 1cm- (½in-) thick rings
chutney (see page 135), to serve
salt

In a mixing bowl, make a runny batter with the gram flour and 250ml (9fl oz) of water. Next, add the turmeric, chilli powder, fresh coriander, baking powder or bicarbonate of soda and salt. Heat enough of the oil in a *karai* or wok-like pan to deep-fry the vegetables. Dip the vegetables into the batter, slice by slice, and deep-fry them in the oil, removing them as they become golden brown. Drain on kitchen paper and serve immediately with the chutney.

SWEET-CORN BHAJIYAS
Deep-fried sweet-corn fritters

115g (4oz) sweet corn, fresh or frozen
2 tablespoons natural yogurt
2 green chillies, deseeded and finely chopped
15g (½oz) finely chopped fresh coriander leaves
¼ teaspoon turmeric

3 tablespoons gram flour (besan; see Stockists), plus a little extra if needed
oil, for deep-frying
chutney (see page 135), to serve
salt

Place the sweet corn in a pan filled with boiling water and boil until tender. Meanwhile, in a mixing bowl, combine the yogurt, chillies, fresh coriander, turmeric, gram flour and salt. Add the sweet corn to this mixture and mash it all together. It should hold together well; add more gram flour if it is too runny. Next, heat enough of the oil in a *karai* or wok-like pan to deep-fry the *bhajiyas*. Make small balls 5cm (2in) in diameter from the mixture, then deep-fry them until golden brown, turning them to ensure they are properly cooked. Drain on kitchen paper and serve immediately with the chutney.

ONION BHAJIYAS
Deep-fried onion fritters

These are called *pyajus* in India ('*pyaz*' is the Hindi word for onions), but in the UK they are incorrectly referred to as *bhajis* (which means 'vegetables', and is a corruption of *bhajiyas*). If you order an onion *bhaji* (as opposed to *bhajiya*) in India, be prepared for quizzical looks, because you are literally ordering onion vegetables!

225g (8oz) gram flour (besan; see Stockists), plus a little extra if needed
pinch turmeric
pinch chilli powder
15g (½oz) finely chopped fresh coriander leaves
¼ teaspoon baking powder or bicarbonate of soda
3 medium onions, peeled and sliced or coarsely chopped
oil, for deep-frying
chutney (see page 135), to serve
salt

In a mixing bowl, make a thick batter with the gram flour and 200ml (7fl oz) of water. Add the turmeric, chilli powder, fresh coriander, baking powder or bicarbonate of soda and salt and combine. The batter should be a thick mixture that holds together well; add more gram flour if it is too runny and more water if it is too thick.

Add the onions and combine. Then heat enough of the oil in a *karai* or wok-like pan to deep-fry the *bhajiyas*. Meanwhile, form the batter into small balls about 5cm (2in) in diameter.

Deep-fry until golden brown, turning several times to ensure they are properly cooked. Drain on kitchen paper and serve immediately with the chutney.

PAPRI CHAAT
Puris topped with potatoes and chutney

In India, these affordable snacky foods are sold by the side of roads, and people on their way home from work will stop to have a little something to tide them over before dinner. *Sev* resembles bits of vermicelli and is made with gram flour. *Chaat masala* is a ready-made powder whose ingredients include mango powder, coriander seeds, black pepper, cloves, chilli powder, ground ginger, dried pomegranate seeds, dried mint leaves and asafoetida (dried gum resin; it takes on a garlicky flavour when cooked). *Chaat* is an Indian term for snacky food, and in India people have *chaat* parties (the concept is similar to Spanish tapas) at which they serve a range of dishes, including this one.

85g (3oz) mung beans
2 medium potatoes
about 16 small crispy puris (crisp flour discs; see Stockists)
200ml (7fl oz) natural yogurt with a pouring consistency
4 tablespoons mitha (date and tamarind) chutney (see page 135)
100g (3½oz) fine sev (see Stockists)
pinch chaat masala powder (see Stockists)
pinch chilli powder
pinch cumin powder
15g (½oz) finely chopped fresh coriander leaves
salt

Soak the beans overnight, or for at least 2 hours, then drain and boil in plenty of salted water for 8-9 minutes – the beans should be firm but cooked. Drain again and set aside. Boil the potatoes in their skins in a pan of boiling salted water until tender, then drain, cool, peel and slice them. Set aside. Arrange the *puris* on a large flat plate, and divide the potato slices between them. Sprinkle over the mung beans, then dribble over the yogurt and chutney. To serve, dust with the *sev*, *chaat masala*, chilli and cumin powders, and garnish with the fresh coriander.

TANDOORI CAULIFLOWER
Marinated cauliflower with a chargrilled flavour

2 teaspoons chaat masala powder (see Stockists)
2 tablespoons lemon juice
1 small cauliflower, weighing about 450g (1lb), divided into florets
6 tablespoons gram flour (besan; see Stockists)
¼ teaspoon red chilli powder

15g (½oz) finely chopped fresh coriander leaves
oil, for deep-frying
lemon wedges, to serve
pudina (mint) chutney (see page 135), to serve
salt

Combine the *chaat masala* powder, the lemon juice and salt, and marinate the cauli-flower in this mixture for 20 minutes. Make a batter with the gram flour, 6 tablespoons of water, salt, the chilli powder and fresh coriander. This should be thick but still a bit runny (viscous, like honey).

Heat enough of the oil in a *karai* or wok-like pan to deep-fry the florets. Dip each one in the batter and fry over a low heat until almost cooked. Remove, drain on kitchen paper and cool. Preheat a grill and grill the florets until golden brown. Garnish with the lemon wedges and serve with the chutney.

CHICKEN TIKKAS
Chicken pieces marinated in yogurt and spices

4 tablespoons natural yogurt
1 tablespoon chicken tikka masala powder (see Stockists)
2 teaspoons puréed ginger
2 teaspoons puréed garlic/10 cloves garlic, peeled and crushed
1 teaspoon chilli powder
pinch powdered orange food colouring dissolved in 1 teaspoon warm water or 1 teaspoon liquid orange food colouring
900g (2lb) boneless chicken, cut into 5cm (2in) cubes
1 piece charcoal
2 tablespoons oil
¼ teaspoon garam masala powder (see Stockists)
15g (½oz) finely chopped fresh coriander leaves
onion rings, to garnish
salt

In an ovenproof dish with a tightly fitting lid combine some salt, the natural yogurt, chicken *tikka masala* powder, ginger, garlic, chilli powder and the orange food colour-ing. Coat the chicken in this marinade and set aside for at least 2 hours. Preheat the oven to 200°C, 400°F, gas mark 6.

Heat the piece of charcoal until it is red hot, then place it in the middle of the marinated chicken and pour the oil on top of the charcoal – it will begin to smoke. Quickly cover the dish with the lid or some kitchen foil, to prevent the smoke escaping, and leave it for 15 minutes, until the smoke has permeated the chicken. Remove the piece of charcoal and cook the chicken pieces in the oven until tender (about 20 minutes). Alternatively, the chicken pieces can be threaded on to skewers and cooked on a barbecue.

To serve, sprinkle with the *garam masala* powder and garnish with the fresh coriander and onion rings. The chicken *tikkas* can be frozen for up to 1 month and reheated in an oven preheated to 200°C, 400°F, gas mark 6 or under a hot grill.

CHICKEN MALAI KEBABS
Creamy chicken kebabs

This unusual starter includes that great British staple, cheddar cheese, as well as cream. These are mild and appeal to those as yet uninitiated in the joys of spicy Indian food.

2 tablespoons puréed garlic/30 cloves garlic, peeled and crushed
1 tablespoon puréed ginger
2 teaspoons freshly ground black pepper
900g (2lb) boneless chicken, cut into 5cm (2in) cubes
2 eggs
3 green chillies, deseeded and finely chopped
85g (3oz) grated cheddar cheese
15g (½oz) chopped fresh coriander leaves
2 tablespoons cornflour
100ml (3½fl oz) single cream
oil, for basting
pudina (mint) or nariyal (coconut) chutney (see page 135), to serve
salt

In a mixing bowl, combine the garlic, ginger, black pepper and salt and add the chicken, coating it in the marinade. Leave for 30 minutes. In a separate bowl, whisk the eggs, then add the green chillies, cheese, fresh coriander and cornflour. Add this mixture to the chicken and leave for at least 2 hours.

After this time, add the single cream to the marinade and leave for 10 minutes. Meanwhile, preheat the oven to 200°C, 400°F, gas mark 6. Thread the chicken pieces on to skewers and cook in the preheated oven for 10 minutes, turning them over halfway through. Alternatively, grill them on a barbecue for about 10 minutes, turning them over halfway through.

Either way, remove after 10 minutes, baste with the oil and return to the oven, or barbecue, for another 5 minutes, until tender, once again turning them over halfway through. Serve with either chutney.

ALOO CHAAP
Seasoned mincemeat encased in mashed potato

These seem to appeal to people of all ages, and are not unlike potato croquettes, but stuffed with mince. In India we always used to eat them with Worcester sauce.

> *4 medium potatoes, weighing about 750g (1lb 10oz)*
> *4 tablespoons oil, plus extra for shallow-frying*
> *1 medium onion, peeled and finely chopped*
> *450g (1lb) minced beef or lamb*
> *1 teaspoon puréed ginger*
> *1 teaspoon puréed garlic/5 cloves garlic, peeled and crushed*
> *1 green chilli, deseeded and finely chopped*
> *2 tablespoons coriander-cumin powder*
> *15g (½oz) finely chopped fresh coriander leaves*
> *¼ teaspoon garam masala powder (see Stockists)*
> *1 teaspoon lemon juice*
> *1 egg, beaten*
> *55g (2oz) breadcrumbs*
> *salt*

First cook the potatoes in their skins in a pan of boiling salted water until tender, then drain, cool, peel and mash them. Set aside. Heat the 4 tablespoons of oil and fry the onion until brown at the edges. Add the mince, ginger, garlic, green chilli, coriander-cumin powder and about 100ml (3½fl oz) of water, to prevent burning. The mince will take about 20 minutes to cook and should be dry.

Next, add the fresh coriander, *garam masala* powder, lemon juice and salt. Season the mashed potato with salt and roll half of it into 6 balls. Each portion should then be flattened and a little of the mince placed in the centre, then covered with the remaining mashed potato and shaped to form fairly flat discs. Dip them in the egg, then coat with the breadcrumbs. In a large flat frying pan, heat enough of the oil to shallow-fry the *chaaps* and fry each one for 5 minutes, turning over halfway through, to give a nice brown crispy coating. Drain on kitchen paper and serve immediately.

ALOO VADAS
Spicy potato balls in batter

> *4 medium potatoes, weighing about 750g (1lb 10oz)*
> *1 green chilli, deseeded and finely chopped*

1 tablespoon lemon juice

½ teaspoon chilli powder

15g (½oz) finely chopped fresh coriander leaves

225g (8oz) gram flour (besan; see Stockists)

oil, for deep-frying

chutney (see page 135), to serve

salt

First cook the potatoes in their skins in a pan of boiling salted water until tender, then drain, cool, peel and mash them. Add the green chilli, lemon juice, chilli powder, fresh coriander and salt and roll the mixture into small balls the size of golf balls. Next, make a batter with the gram flour, a quarter of a teaspoon of salt and 250ml (9fl oz) of water. It should be of a consistency that is easy to dip into to coat the balls. Heat enough of the oil in *karai* or wok-like pan to deep-fry the potato balls. Dip the balls in the batter, then deep-fry until golden brown. Drain on kitchen paper and serve with the chutney.

SHAMI KEBABS
Stuffed lentil kebabs

These can be wrapped in chapatis (flat bread) or tortillas and served with chutney and salad. You can freeze the kebabs for up to 1 month and fry them before serving.

125g (4½oz) chana daal (golden yellow lentils; see Stockists)

450g (1lb) minced beef or lamb

2 each of cardamom pods, cinnamon sticks, bay leaves and cloves (whole garam masala)

2 onions, peeled, 1 roughly chopped and 1 finely chopped

25g (1oz) finely chopped fresh coriander leaves

2 green chillies, deseeded

1 raw egg

1 teaspoon puréed ginger

1 teaspoon puréed garlic/5 cloves garlic, peeled and crushed

¼ teaspoon garam masala powder (see Stockists)

1 hard-boiled egg, finely chopped

oil, for shallow-frying

onion rings, lemon wedges and fresh mint, to serve (optional)

salt

Soak the daal overnight or for at least 3 hours, and drain. Then boil it in plenty of boiling water for 12-15 minutes, drain and set aside. Cook the mince, whole *garam masala* and salt in 400ml (14fl oz) water until well cooked. The mixture is meant to be fairly dry, but top up with water if it gets very dry during cooking. Put the daal and mince in a blender together with the roughly chopped onion, half the fresh coriander, the green chillies and raw egg. Blend until smooth. Add the ginger, garlic and *garam masala* powder to this mixture and set aside. In a separate bowl, mix together the boiled egg, finely chopped onion and remaining fresh coriander. Shape half the meat mixture into flat rounds about 7.5cm (3in) in diameter and place some of the egg and onion mixture in the centre of each. Cover with the remaining kebab mixture and shape into small patties (like fish cakes). Next, heat enough of the oil in a frying pan to shallow-fry the kebabs. Shallow-fry them for 7 minutes, turning them once halfway through, until browned and slightly crisp on the outside. You can serve these garnished with the onion rings, lemon wedges and fresh mint.

SEEKH KEBABS
Long kebabs

These long burgers can be as mild or as spicy as you wish, and the raw mixture can be smoked using the *dhuan* technique (see page 28) to impart a wonderful chargrilled flavour. You can freeze them for up to 1 month and grill them before serving.

> *2 tablespoons gram flour (besan; see Stockists)*
> *450g (1lb) minced beef or lamb*
> *2 teaspoons puréed garlic/10 cloves garlic, peeled and crushed*
> *1 teaspoon puréed ginger*
> *2 green chillies, deseeded and finely chopped*
> *2 teaspoons poppy seeds*
> *1 teaspoon cumin powder*
> *¼ teaspoon garam masala powder (see Stockists)*
> *1 medium onion, peeled and finely chopped*
> *15g (½oz) finely chopped fresh coriander leaves*
> *1 egg*
> *hara (green) or pudina (mint) chutney (see page 135), to serve*
> *onion rings, lemon wedges and fresh mint, to serve (optional)*
> *salt*

Preheat the oven to 200°C, 400°F, gas mark 6. First roast the gram flour by heating it in a frying pan for a couple of minutes and stirring it round, then mix the gram flour and all the ingredients, apart from the chutney, onion rings, lemon wedges and fresh mint, together and knead well. Leave to stand for 15 minutes. Moisten your hands with cold water and shape the mixture into 6-8 long kebabs about 15cm (6in) in length. Lay out on a baking tray and cook in the oven for 12 minutes, carefully turning them over halfway through (they are fragile and have a tendency to break). Alternatively they can be threaded on to skewers and cooked on a barbecue. Serve with the chutney. You can garnish them with the onion rings, fresh mint and lemon wedges.

RESHMI KEBABS
Delicate chicken kebabs

> *2 eggs*
> *1 tablespoon cumin powder*
> *1 teaspoon chilli powder*
> *1 teaspoon freshly ground black pepper*
> *2 tablespoons oil*
> *900g (2lb) chicken mince*
> *85g (3oz) ground cashew nuts*
> *2 tablespoons puréed ginger*
> *1 onion, peeled and finely chopped*
> *15g (½oz) finely chopped fresh coriander leaves*
> *¼ teaspoon garam masala powder (see Stockists)*
> *butter, to baste*
> *onion rings, lemon wedges and fresh mint, to serve (optional)*
> *salt*

Beat the eggs in a mixing bowl and add the cumin powder, chilli powder, black pepper, oil and salt. Add the mince, mix well and leave for about 15 minutes. Then add the cashew nuts, ginger, onion, fresh coriander and *garam masala* powder. Mix well. Divide into 12 portions. Preheat the grill to medium. Thread each portion on to a skewer, elongating each one to span most of the length of the skewer, and wetting your hands to ease the process. Grill for 5 minutes, until golden brown, turning once halfway through. Baste with the butter before serving. You can serve these garnished with the onion rings, lemon wedges and fresh mint. You can freeze them for up to 1 month and grill them before serving.

MEAT CUTLETS
Hamburgers with a difference

When I was a young girl we often ate these with chips. Leftovers make great sandwiches, which are particularly good for picnics. You can freeze them for up to 1 month and reheat them in an oven preheated to 200°C, 400°F, gas mark 6 before serving.

450g (1lb) minced beef or lamb

2 green chillies, deseeded and finely chopped

2 medium onions, peeled and finely chopped

15g (½oz) finely chopped fresh coriander leaves

1 teaspoon puréed garlic/5 cloves garlic, peeled and crushed

1 teaspoon puréed ginger

1 egg, beaten

55g [2oz] breadcrumbs

oil, for shallow-frying

salt

In a bowl, mix the mince with the green chillies, onions, fresh coriander, garlic, ginger and salt. Knead the mixture together for a few minutes, then set aside for 30 minutes. Form the mixture into 4 flat round cutlets the size of the palm of your hand – they should be thinner than hamburgers.

Dip the cutlets in the egg, then coat with the breadcrumbs. Next, in a large frying pan, heat enough of the oil to shallow-fry the cutlets and fry them for 5 minutes on each side. Drain well on kitchen paper before serving.

VEGETABLE CUTLETS

4 medium potatoes, weighing about 750g (1lb 10oz)

115g (4oz) mixed vegetables (such as sweet corn, peas, beans and carrots), boiled

1 green chilli, deseeded and finely chopped

15g (½oz) finely chopped fresh coriander leaves

1 teaspoon puréed ginger

1 medium onion, peeled and finely chopped

1 tablespoon lemon juice

1 egg, beaten

55g (2oz) breadcrumbs

oil, for shallow-frying

salt

First cook the potatoes in their skins in a pan of boiling salted water until tender, then drain, cool, peel and mash them. Combine well with the vegetables, green chilli, fresh coriander, ginger, onion, lemon juice and salt, then shape the mixture into cutlets the size of the palm of your hand.

Dip the cutlets into the egg, then coat with the breadcrumbs. Next, in a large frying pan, heat enough of the oil to shallow-fry them, and shallow-fry on both sides, until golden brown. Drain well on kitchen paper before serving.

DAHI VADAS
Lentil donuts with yogurt and chutney

These should be light and fluffy and smothered in yogurt. The secret is to beat the lentil mixture well in order to make the *vadas* light and spongy.

> 225g (8oz) urad daal (tiny white split lentils; see Stockists)
> ¼ teaspoon garam masala powder (see Stockists)
> ¼ teaspoon freshly ground black pepper
> oil, for deep-frying
> ½ teaspoon lemon juice
> 500g (1lb 2oz) natural yogurt
> ½ teaspoon sugar
> mitha (date and tamarind) chutney (see page 135), to serve
> 1 teaspoon cumin powder
> ¼ teaspoon chilli powder
> 15g (½oz) finely chopped fresh coriander leaves
> salt

Soak the *urad* daal overnight, or for at least for 4 hours. Drain, then process to a fine paste in a food processor or blender, adding a couple of tablespoons of water. Add the *garam masala* powder, salt and black pepper and beat with your hands for 10 minutes, until the mixture is fairly light. A wooden spoon can be used if the hand beating proves difficult! Heat enough of the oil in a *karai* or wok-like pan to deep-fry the *vadas*. Meanwhile, make small balls the size of golf balls from the mixture and lightly flatten each one before frying, then deep-fry until light brown. Now add salt and the lemon juice to a large bowl of cold water and put the fried *vadas* into this. Leave for 2 minutes, then remove, gently squeezing out the water using the palms of both your hands, and lay them out on a serving dish. Whisk the yogurt with a little salt and the sugar, adding a little water if the yogurt is too thick – the consistency should be that of double cream that has not been whipped. To serve, cover the *vadas* with the yogurt and *mitha* chutney, and garnish with the cumin powder, chilli powder and fresh coriander.

ALOO TIKKIS
Potato patties stuffed with peas and spices

Street-food vendors all over India serve these with *ragda*, a dish consisting of chickpeas in a sauce, and so these are also known as *ragda* patties.

> 4 medium potatoes, weighing about 750g (1lb 10oz)

15g (½oz) finely chopped fresh coriander leaves

25g (1oz) cornflour

85g (3oz) peas

oil, for shallow-frying

½ teaspoon cumin seeds

2 teaspoons coriander-cumin powder

½ teaspoon chilli powder

1 green chilli, deseeded and chopped

pudina (mint) or mitha (date and tamarind) chutney (see page 135), to serve

salt

First cook the potatoes in their skins in a pan of boiling salted water until tender, then drain, cool, peel and mash them, adding the fresh coriander, salt and cornflour to the mixture. Mix well, then divide the mixture into small balls the size of golf balls. Next, cook the peas in a pan of boiling salted water until tender; drain and set aside. Heat 2 tablespoons of the oil in a pan. When the oil is very hot, add a couple of the cumin seeds. If they crackle and turn a darker shade, immediately add the rest. If they turn very dark, reduce the heat and add the remaining cumin seeds after 1 minute. Add the peas and coriander-cumin powder, chilli powder and green chilli and stir well for 2 minutes. Remove the mixture from the heat, cool, then mash it all together. Take the potato balls, flatten them, and place a small portion of the pea filling in the centre of each. Encase the filling in the surrounding potato and form into small patties the shape of small fish cakes. Then heat 4 tablespoons of the oil in a frying pan and shallow-fry them until golden brown. Remove, drain on kitchen paper and serve with the chutney.

PANEER TIKKAS
Curd cheese morsels

When I was a growing up in India, *paneer* was always made at home. Today it can be bought ready-prepared from Indian shops, but it is quite tasteless eaten on its own and should be cooked and seasoned. Ajowan (sometimes referred to as carom), a spice commonly used in Indian cuisine, is said to taste of a combination of anise and oregano with a hint of black pepper. These flavoursome *paneer* morsels make an excellent vegetarian dish (*paneer* is a good source of protein), and can be smothered in the creamy sauce used for chicken *tikka masala* (see page 95) to make *paneer tikka masala*.

1 teaspoon cumin powder

1 teaspoon ajowan (carom) seeds (see Stockists)

¼ teaspoon turmeric

¼ teaspoon freshly ground black pepper

¼ teaspoon garam masala powder (see Stockists]

450g (1lb) paneer (see Stockists), cut into 2.5cm (1in) cubes

1 egg

1 tablespoon gram flour (besan; see Stockists)

3 tablespoons double cream

1 onion, peeled and quartered

1 tablespoon butter, melted

pudina (mint) chutney (see page 135), to serve

salt

Combine the spices and some salt in a bowl, add the *paneer*, coat it in the mixture and set aside for 20 minutes. Beat the egg in another bowl and add the gram flour and cream. Add the *paneer* (with all the spices) and the onion and set aside for 1 hour. Preheat the grill to medium and thread the *paneer* and onion quarters on to skewers. Grill for 10-12 minutes, turning over halfway through (they should be speckled brown), then brush with the butter. Serve with the chutney.

SMOKED SALMON TIKKAS
Smoked salmon morsels

This is one of my favourite dishes. You can freeze the salmon pieces for up to 1 month and reheat them in an oven preheated to 200°C, 400°F, gas mark 6 before serving.

900g (2lb) salmon fillets

2 tablespoons lemon juice

1 tablespoon puréed ginger

1 tablespoon puréed garlic/15 cloves garlic, peeled and crushed

2 tablespoons hara masala (chilli and coriander paste; see page 31)

1 teaspoon chilli powder

15g (½oz) chopped fresh dill

¼ teaspoon freshly ground black pepper

1 large piece charcoal

4 green cardamom pods

4 tablespoons oil

15g (½oz) finely chopped fresh coriander leaves

lemon slices, to garnish

salt

Cut the salmon into pieces about 5cm (2in) square and transfer to an ovenproof dish with a tightly fitting lid. In a mixing bowl combine all the ingredients, except the charcoal, cardamom pods, oil, fresh coriander and lemon slices, starting with the lemon juice and 1 teaspoon of salt, and add to the salmon. Set aside to marinate for at least 30 minutes. After this time, heat the charcoal until it is red hot, and place it in the middle of the fish. Place the cardamom pods on top of the charcoal and pour over 2 tablespoons of the oil – the charcoal will begin to smoke. Cover immediately with the lid or some kitchen foil and leave for 15 minutes, then remove the charcoal and cardamom pods.

Heat the remaining oil in a frying pan and pan-fry the salmon pieces on both sides over a high heat for a few minutes. The outside of the fish should be speckled brown. Alternatively, cook the *tikkas* in an oven preheated to 200°C, 400°F, gas mark 6 for 10-12 minutes, turning once halfway through. Garnish with the fresh coriander and serve with the slices of lemon.

VEGETABLES AND VEGETARIAN

Sesame potatoes, cauliflower with ginger and cumin, lentils infused with garlic... Simple vegetable dishes, exotic spices – the ideal accompaniments to any meal or perfect as the main meal itself.

MASALA WALE ALOO
Spicy Bombay potatoes

In India, this is often served at high teas – buffet parties, beginning at about 5.30pm, at which tea and dishes such as kebabs and *bhajiyas* (deep-fried vegetable fritters) are served. You can use any variety of potato, though my preference is for new potatoes. To make it really special, use whole coriander and cumin seeds and whole dried red chillies, roughly ground in a coffee grinder or with a pestle and mortar, instead of ready-made powders.

> *4 large potatoes, weighing about 1.25kg (2lb 2oz; or similar weight new potatoes)*
> *1 teaspoon chilli powder*
> *1½ tablespoons coriander-cumin powder*
> *¼ teaspoon turmeric*
> *1 tablespoon tomato purée*
> *4 tablespoons oil*
> *6 curry leaves*
> *½ teaspoon black mustard seeds*
> *2 teaspoons puréed garlic/10 cloves garlic, peeled and crushed*
> *2 green chillies, slit down the middle*
> *1 tablespoon lemon juice*
> *15g (½oz) finely chopped fresh coriander leaves*
> *salt*

First cook the potatoes in their skins in a pan of boiling salted water until tender. Drain, cool, peel and cut them into 2.5cm (1in) cubes (if using new potatoes, simply cut in half). Set aside. Mix the chilli powder, coriander-cumin powder, turmeric and tomato purée with a tablespoon of water and set aside. (This is the *masala* mixture.) Heat the oil in a large frying pan and, when it is very hot, drop in a curry leaf. If it sizzles and turns a darker shade, add all the other leaves and the mustard seeds. If the leaf turns very dark, reduce the heat and add the remaining curry leaves and mustard seeds after 1 minute. As soon as the seeds start to pop, add the garlic, the *masala* mixture and 125ml (4fl oz) of water. Stir for a few minutes over a high heat. Add the potatoes, salt and green chillies, then lower the heat and cook for 2 minutes. Add the lemon juice, garnish with the fresh coriander and serve immediately.

TILWALE ALOO
Potatoes with sesame seeds

Potatoes are a great favourite all over India, as well as being a staple food. Readily available throughout the year, they are cooked in myriad ways. This lovely recipe has the nutty flavour of sesame and cumin seeds, with the wonderful tang of lemon as well.

4 large potatoes, weighing about 1.25kg (2lb 2oz)
4 tablespoons oil
6 curry leaves
1 teaspoon cumin seeds
2 dried red chillies
3 cloves
1 teaspoon sesame seeds
½ teaspoon chilli powder
2 teaspoons coriander-cumin powder
¼ teaspoon turmeric
1 teaspoon puréed garlic/5 cloves garlic, peeled and crushed
1 teaspoon lemon juice
15g (½oz) finely chopped fresh coriander leaves
salt

First cook the potatoes in their skins in a pan of boiling salted water, until tender. Drain, cool, peel and dice them. Next, heat the oil in a large frying pan. When it is very hot, drop in a curry leaf. If it sizzles and turns a darker shade, add all the other leaves and the cumin seeds. If the leaf turns very dark, reduce the heat and add the remaining curry leaves and cumin seeds after 1 minute. Then add the dried red chillies, cloves, sesame seeds, chilli powder, coriander-cumin powder, turmeric and garlic. Add a tablespoon of water to prevent burning, then add the potatoes and stir. Add salt and the lemon juice, then leave to cook for 5 minutes, ensuring the potato pieces are all coated with the spices. When they are ready, garnish with the fresh coriander and serve.

GUJARATI-STYLE POTATOES
Potatoes with a hint of lemon and sugar

A mild sweet-sour dish tempered with curry leaves and fresh coriander, this is a perfect accompaniment for plain lamb chops or roast chicken.

4 large potatoes, weighing about 1.25kg (2lb 2oz)
4 tablespoons oil
5 curry leaves
½ teaspoon mustard seeds
1 green chilli, deseeded and chopped
¼ teaspoon turmeric

½ teaspoon sugar

1 tablespoon lemon juice

15g (½oz) finely chopped fresh coriander leaves

salt

First cook the potatoes in their skins in a pan of boiling salted water, until tender. Drain, cool, peel and dice them. Heat the oil in a large frying pan. When it is very hot, drop in a curry leaf. If it sizzles and turns a darker shade, add all the other leaves and the mustard seeds. If the leaf turns very dark, reduce the heat and add the remaining curry leaves and mustard seeds after 1 minute. Reduce the heat (if you haven't already) and add the green chilli, potatoes, turmeric and salt. Stir for a few minutes, coating all the potatoes in the spices. Add the sugar and lemon juice, garnish with the fresh coriander and serve hot or cold.

SAG ALOO
Spinach with potatoes

A rustic dish of leafy spinach and new potatoes with their skins left on, this is best eaten with chapatis (flat bread).

10 small new potatoes

4 tablespoons oil

3 shallots, peeled and thinly sliced

½ teaspoon chilli powder

¼ teaspoon turmeric

1 tablespoon coriander-cumin powder

1 teaspoon puréed ginger

1 teaspoon puréed garlic/5 cloves garlic, peeled and crushed

450g (1lb) leafy spinach

1 tablespoon lemon juice

15g (½oz) finely chopped fresh coriander leaves

salt

First cook the potatoes in their skins in a pan of boiling salted water, until tender. Drain, cool and halve them. Heat the oil in a large frying pan and fry the shallots until golden brown. Add the chilli powder, turmeric, coriander-cumin powder, ginger and garlic, along with a tablespoon of water, and fry for a few minutes. Add the potatoes and continue to fry for 2 more minutes, adding salt. Next, add the spinach and leave it to cook for a few minutes, until wilted, adding a small amount of water if the mixture looks very dry. Then stir in the lemon juice and garnish with the fresh coriander, to serve.

ALOO GOBI
Potatoes with cauliflower

This simple recipe is popular in India in the winter, when cauliflower is plentiful. Peas can be added, for variety. This fairly dry dish is best eaten with chapatis (flat bread).

> *4 medium potatoes, weighing about 750g (1lb 10oz)*
> *4 tablespoons oil*
> *6 curry leaves*
> *1 tablespoon whole cumin seeds*
> *1 small cauliflower, cut into florets*
> *1 tablespoon coriander-cumin powder*
> *¼ teaspoon turmeric*
> *½ teaspoon chilli powder*
> *1 green chilli, deseeded and finely chopped*
> *1 teaspoon puréed ginger*
> *1 tomato, chopped*
> *1 teaspoon lemon juice*
> *15g (½oz) finely chopped fresh coriander leaves*
> *salt*

First parboil the potatoes in their skins in a pan of boiling salted water for about 7 minutes. Drain, cool, peel and dice them. Heat the oil in a *karai* or other wok-like pan. When it is very hot, drop in a curry leaf. If it sizzles and turns a darker shade, add all the other leaves and the cumin seeds. If the leaf turns very dark, reduce the heat and add the remaining curry leaves and cumin seeds after 1 minute. Lower the heat (if you haven't already), add the cauliflower and fry for a few minutes. Add the potatoes and all the other ingredients, except the lemon juice and fresh coriander, and continue to fry for a few more minutes. Then add 250ml (9fl oz) of water and leave to cook over a low heat until the vegetables are tender (about 20 minutes). Add the lemon juice and garnish with the fresh coriander, to serve. This is meant to be a fairly dry dish, but if you prefer a bit more sauce, add a little more water.

ALOO, MATTAR AUR TAMATAR
Potatoes, peas and tomatoes

A simple dish, which we often had in winter when peas and tomatoes were available in abundance. Best served with chapatis (flat bread) or *puris* (deep-fried bread).

> *4 tablespoons oil*

2 medium onions, peeled and finely chopped
¼ teaspoon turmeric
1 teaspoon chilli powder
1 tablespoon coriander-cumin powder
4 plum tomatoes (preferably tinned, for better colour)
1 tablespoon tomato purée
4 medium potatoes, weighing about 750g (1lb 10oz), peeled and cubed
250g (9oz) peas, fresh or frozen
15g (½oz) finely chopped fresh coriander leaves
salt

Heat the oil in a saucepan and fry the onions until translucent and brown at the edges. Add all the spices and fry for 2 minutes with the tomatoes, tomato purée and salt. Add the potatoes together with 250ml (9fl oz) of water and leave to cook until the potatoes are tender. Then add the peas and leave to simmer for a couple more minutes, until the peas are tender, adding more water if necessary. This is a fairly dry dish, but if you prefer more sauce, add a bit more water. To serve, garnish with the fresh coriander.

QUICK SPICY SWEET CORN

This is one of those fantastic last-minute recipes – most of us usually have a bag of sweet corn lurking somewhere in the freezer, and this dish can be rustled up quickly at short notice, when guests turn up unexpectedly. It is delicious with hot pitta bread – another freezer staple. *Panchporan* is the Indian equivalent of Chinese five-spice (*panch* means 'five'), and contains mustard seeds, cumin seeds, black onion seeds, fenugreek seeds and fennel seeds mixed in equal proportions.

3 tablespoons oil
6 curry leaves
½ teaspoon panchporan (see Stockists)
¼ teaspoon turmeric
½ teaspoon chilli powder
1 tablespoon coriander-cumin powder
1 teaspoon puréed garlic/5 cloves garlic, peeled and crushed
2 tablespoons tomato purée
450g (1lb) frozen sweet corn
15g (½oz) finely chopped fresh coriander leaves
salt

Heat the oil in a saucepan. When it is very hot, drop in a curry leaf. If it sizzles and turns a darker shade, add all the other leaves. If the leaf turns very dark, reduce the heat and add the remaining curry leaves after 1 minute. Remove the pan from the heat.

Add the *panchporan*, turmeric, chilli powder, coriander-cumin powder, garlic, tomato purée and salt. Return the pan to the heat and add the sweet corn and 300ml (10fl oz) of water. Bring the mixture to the boil and let it simmer until the sweet corn is tender. If more sauce is preferred, add a bit more water. To serve, garnish with the fresh coriander.

QUICK GREEN BEANS

Beans can be cooked in so many different ways, and this is one of the simplest and most delicious ways to use them. *Panchporan* (Indian five-spice, *see previous recipe*), adds zest.

> *3 tablespoons oil*
> *6 curry leaves (preferably fresh)*
> *1 teaspoon panchporan (see Stockists)*
> *1 teaspoon puréed garlic/5 cloves garlic, peeled and crushed*
> *¼ teaspoon turmeric*
> *¼ teaspoon chilli powder*
> *450g (1lb) beans, fresh or frozen, trimmed (if using fresh, parboil first)*
> *15g (½oz) finely chopped fresh coriander leaves*
> *salt*

Heat the oil in a saucepan. When it is very hot, drop in a curry leaf. If it sizzles and turns a darker shade, add all the other leaves and the *panchporan*. If the leaf turns very dark, reduce the heat and add the remaining curry leaves and *panchporan* after 1 minute. Add the garlic, turmeric and chilli powder, followed by the green beans, then add 300ml (10fl oz) of water and some salt. Bring to the boil and leave to simmer until the beans are tender. To serve, garnish with the fresh coriander.

QUICK MIXED VEGETABLES

This simple, versatile dish is ideal as a side dish for any Indian meat or chicken preparation. It can also be served with plain lamb chops or roast chicken.

> *3 tablespoons oil*
> *6-8 curry leaves*
> *1 teaspoon black mustard seeds*
> *1 tablespoon puréed garlic/15 cloves garlic, peeled and crushed*

1 tablespoon coriander-cumin powder

¼ teaspoon chilli powder

¼ teaspoon turmeric

1 tablespoon tomato purée

450g (1lb) mixed vegetables (such as sweet corn, peas, beans and carrots), fresh or frozen, chopped

15g (½oz) finely chopped fresh coriander leaves

salt

Heat the oil in a saucepan. When it is very hot, drop in a curry leaf. If it sizzles and turns a darker shade, add all the other leaves and the mustard seeds. If the leaf turns very dark, reduce the heat and add the remaining curry leaves and mustard seeds after 1 minute. Add the garlic, coriander-cumin powder, chilli powder and turmeric and stir for 2 minutes. Then, add the tomato purée and mixed vegetables together with the salt and 300ml (10fl oz) of water. Bring to the boil and leave to simmer for 5 minutes. If a drier sauce is preferred, continue to cook over a high for a few minutes to evaporate the water. To serve, garnish with the fresh coriander.

MUSHROOM DO PYAZA
Mushrooms with onions

Mushrooms were not common when I was growing up in India. Today, together with asparagus and baby corn, they have become very popular at sophisticated weddings and in restaurants. It is still rare to find mushrooms served on a daily basis in the home.

4 tablespoons oil

3 medium onions, peeled, 2 finely chopped and 1 coarsely chopped

1 tablespoon coriander-cumin powder

¼ teaspoon chilli powder

¼ teaspoon turmeric

2 teaspoons puréed garlic/10 cloves garlic, peeled and crushed

1 teaspoon puréed ginger

1 green chilli, deseeded and chopped

1 tablespoon tomato purée

450g (1lb) sliced mushrooms

pinch garam masala powder (see Stockists)

15g (½oz) finely chopped fresh coriander leaves

salt

Heat the oil in a saucepan and fry the finely chopped onions until golden brown. Add all the spices (except the *garam masala* powder), the garlic, ginger, green chilli and the tomato purée, along with a tablespoon of water to prevent the spices burning. Fry over a high heat until you can see the oil begin to separate from the spices at the edges of the pan, adding a little water from time to time to prolong the frying and stop the spices sticking and burning. Next, add the coarsely chopped onion, mushrooms and salt, and fry for 2 more minutes. Add 500ml (18fl oz) of water and leave to cook over a medium heat. If a thinner sauce is preferred, add more water. Once the mushrooms are tender, sprinkle over the *garam masala* powder and garnish with the fresh coriander, to serve.

CHANA BATATA
Chickpeas and potatoes

This is a favourite among the Khoja community, and the East African Ismailis enjoy it with *chevda* – a snack made from a mixture of fried puffed rice, peanuts, cashew nuts and *sev* (gram-flour vermicelli) sprinkled on top. It's a wonderful mid-evening snack.

> *2 medium potatoes, weighing about 400g (14oz)*
> *3 tablespoons oil*
> *6 curry leaves*
> *1 teaspoon mustard seeds*
> *1 green chilli, slit down the middle*
> *½ teaspoon chilli powder*
> *¼ teaspoon turmeric*
> *2 tablespoons tomato purée*
> *1 teaspoon puréed ginger*
> *800g (1lb 12oz) tinned chickpeas*
> *1 teaspoon sugar*
> *1 tablespoon lemon juice*
> *15g (½oz) finely chopped fresh coriander leaves*
> *salt*

First boil the potatoes in their skins in a pan of boiling salted water until tender. Drain, cool, peel and dice them. Heat the oil in a saucepan. When it is very hot, drop in a curry leaf. If it sizzles and turns a darker shade, add all the other leaves and the mustard seeds. If the leaf turns very dark, reduce the heat and add the remaining curry leaves and the mustard seeds after 1 minute. Lower the heat (if you haven't already) and add the green chilli, chilli powder, turmeric, tomato purée and ginger in quick succession. Next, add the chickpeas, potatoes and some salt, together with 275ml (9½fl oz) of water. Bring to the boil and leave to simmer for 10 minutes. Then add the sugar and lemon juice and combine. To serve, garnish with the fresh coriander.

SOOKHA GOBI
Cauliflower with ginger and cumin

In northern India, cauliflower is often cooked with ginger, which aids digestion.

> 3 tablespoons oil
> 2 tablespoons sliced fresh ginger
> 1 teaspoon cumin seeds
> 1 green chilli, deseeded and chopped
> ¼ teaspoon red chilli powder
> 1 medium cauliflower, cut into florets
> pinch garam masala powder (see Stockists)
> 15g (½oz) finely chopped fresh coriander leaves
> salt

Heat the oil in a large frying pan and fry the ginger for 40 seconds. Add the cumin seeds, green chilli, chilli powder, salt and cauliflower. Stir well, add a tablespoon or two of water, cover and leave to cook over a medium heat until the cauliflower is tender, stirring from time to time. (Transferring the cauliflower to a microwave at this stage, and letting it cook for 6 minutes on full power can speed up the process.) Sprinkle with the *garam masala* powder and fresh coriander before serving.

TARKA DAAL
Lentils infused with garlic

In India the Hindi word daal refers to any member of the legume or pulse family, the most popular types of daal being lentils, such as *chana* (golden yellow lentils), *moong* (split mung beans), *masoor* (red lentils when split; with a brown outer layer when whole) and *toor* (deep yellow lentils). The different types have their own characteristics: some are oily, while others are harder to digest than others (our cook always used to boil daals with ginger, as it is known to counteract flatulence!), and they can either be combined and cooked together, or used individually. It is quite common to add spinach to daals.

A rich source of protein, daals are especially favoured by vegetarians. The thick sauce is delicious with bread dipped in, but if a daal is to be eaten with rice it must be slightly diluted, as the consistency should be more like that of a fairly thick soup. The following recipe, flavoured with a *tarka* (a hot oil or butter infusion) of garlic, cumin seeds and chilli, is one that appeals to most people.

> 225g (8oz) mixed daal (toor, chana and masoor; see Stockists)

¼ teaspoon turmeric
1cm (½in) ginger, peeled
2 tablespoons butter
½ teaspoon cumin seeds
2 cloves garlic, finely sliced
¼ teaspoon chilli powder
15g (½oz) finely chopped fresh coriander leaves
salt

Soak the daals for at least 3 hours, or overnight, then rinse them several times in cold water. Next, boil them in a large pan in 1.2 litres (2 pints) of water with the turmeric, salt and piece of ginger. Keep stirring to prevent sticking, adding more water if the mixture becomes too thick.

When the mixture reaches a soup-like consistency, remove it from the heat, and remove and discard the ginger. In a small pan, melt the butter, and add the cumin seeds and garlic together with the chilli powder. Immediately lift the pan off the heat and pour this butter mixture (the *tarka*) on to the daal (do not stir it in). Cover the pan immediately and allow the flavours to infuse for a few moments. Garnish with the fresh coriander before serving.

MATTAR PANEER
Peas with curd cheese

A rich, tasty vegetarian treat, here cubes of *paneer* (curd cheese) and peas, lavishly flavoured with spices, are simmered until tender in a tomato gravy.

250g (9oz) paneer (see Stockists)
6 tablespoons oil
1 onion, peeled and finely grated
1 teaspoon puréed ginger
1 teaspoon puréed garlic/5 cloves garlic, peeled and crushed
1 tablespoon coriander-cumin powder
¼ teaspoon turmeric
¼ teaspoon chilli powder
1 green chilli, deseeded and finely chopped
1 tablespoon tomato purée, or 2 fresh tomatoes, chopped
2 tablespoons natural yogurt
450g (1lb) peas, fresh or frozen
15g (½oz) finely chopped fresh coriander leaves
salt

Cut the *paneer* into 5cm (2in) cubes. Heat the oil in a frying pan, add the *paneer* and fry until light brown. Remove and set aside. Add the onion to the same oil and fry for a few minutes, until it begins to brown. Add the ginger, garlic, coriander-cumin powder, turmeric, chilli powder and green chilli, together with a tablespoon of water, to prevent sticking and burning. Next, add the tomato purée or fresh tomatoes and fry for a few more minutes. Then, add the yogurt a tablespoon at a time, waiting for the first tablespoon to be fully absorbed before adding the second, and stirring well to prevent curdling. Then add salt, the peas and 125ml (4fl oz) of water, and leave to simmer for 5 minutes. Finally, add the *paneer*, garnish with the fresh coriander and serve.

BHINDI KI BHAJI
Okra with onions

Never add water to okra, as this will lead to it becoming a very sticky mess!

> *4 tablespoons oil*
> *1 teaspoon cumin seeds*
> *2 medium onions, peeled and coarsely chopped*
> *1 teaspoon puréed garlic/5 cloves garlic, peeled and crushed*
> *1 tomato, sliced*
> *¼ teaspoon turmeric*
> *¼ teaspoon chilli powder*
> *1 tablespoon coriander-cumin powder*
> *450g (1lb) fresh okra, chopped (frozen okra is also very good)*
> *15g (½oz) finely chopped fresh coriander leaves*
> *salt*

Heat the oil in a large frying pan. When it is very hot, add a couple of the cumin seeds; if they sizzle and turn darker, add the rest. If they turn very dark, reduce the heat and add the remaining seeds after 1 minute. Add the onions and sauté until translucent. Then add the garlic and sliced tomato, together with the turmeric, chilli powder and coriander-cumin powder, immediately followed by the okra and salt. Stir to avoid sticking. Leave over a low heat and cook until tender (about 15 minutes), stirring frequently. Do not add water, as this will make it sticky. To serve, garnish with the fresh coriander.

NARIYAL WALA BHUTTA
Sweet corn in coconut

This is a favourite among East African Asians, who have seized upon the abundance of coconut in that region to produce some delicious coconut-based recipes. This has a wonderful creamy, tangy sauce, seasoned generously with fresh coriander.

900g (2lb) sweet corn, fresh or frozen
2 small fresh tomatoes, chopped
¼ teaspoon turmeric
½ teaspoon puréed garlic/2-3 cloves garlic, peeled and crushed
2 green chillies, deseeded and chopped
200g (7oz) creamed coconut
4 tablespoons hara masala (chilli and coriander paste; see page 31)
1 tablespoon lemon juice
15g (½oz) finely chopped fresh coriander leaves
salt

Boil the sweet corn in a large pan of boiling salted water until tender. Drain and set aside. Next, bring 568ml (1 pint) of water to the boil and add the tomatoes, turmeric, garlic, green chillies and salt. Then add the creamed coconut, sweet corn and *hara masala*. As soon as the coconut has melted, remove from the pan from the heat, add the lemon juice and fresh coriander and serve. For a thinner sauce, simply add more water.

ANDA KA KHEEMA
Spicy scrambled eggs

Masala omelettes, filled with spices and peppers, were my grandmother's speciality, but this particular dish was our favourite when my siblings and I were growing up. It is a mild dish, which is probably why it appealed to us then, and tastes great with crusty French bread, toast or chapatis (flat bread). A good variation involves frying the onions and potatoes, then breaking the eggs on top, one by one, and baking the whole thing in an oven preheated to 200°C, 400°F, gas mark 6 until the eggs are set.

8 tablespoons oil
2 onions, peeled and coarsely chopped
2 large potatoes, peeled and diced into 1cm (½in) pieces
¼ teaspoon chilli powder
1½ tablespoons coriander-cumin powder
¼ teaspoon turmeric
1 green chilli, deseeded and finely chopped
6 eggs, beaten
15g (½oz) finely chopped fresh coriander leaves
salt (recipe continued on page 73)

Masala wale aloo

black peppercorns

cumin

turmeric

dried fenugreek

bay leaves

saffron

dried red chillies

cloves

cinnamon

cardamom pods

coriander

panchporan

Spices commonly used in Indian cooking

mint

curry leaves

fenugreek

red chillies

garlic

fresh dill

fresh ginger

green chillies

coriander leaves

Key ingredients in Indian cooking

Smoked salmon *tikkas* and naan bread

Machi ka salna and *bhuni khichri*

Karai cicken

*Gosht-e-*Mehboob

Chicken *tikka masala*

Heat the oil in a large frying pan. Add the chopped onions and potatoes and cook until the onions are translucent but not browned and the potatoes are tender. Next, add all the spices, the green chilli and salt and fry for 2-3 minutes. Reduce the heat and add the beaten eggs, stirring constantly. Remove from the heat when the eggs have blended and the mixture is dry. To serve, garnish with the fresh coriander.

VEGETABLE MAKHANWALA
Vegetables in a creamy sauce

3 tablespoons oil

1 onion, peeled and finely grated

4 teaspoons coriander-cumin powder

½ teaspoon chilli powder

¼ teaspoon turmeric

1 teaspoon puréed ginger

1 teaspoon puréed garlic/5 cloves garlic, peeled and crushed

1 tablespoon tomato purée

450g (1lb) mixed vegetables (such as sweet corn, peas, beans and carrots), fresh or frozen, chopped and boiled

1 tablespoon ground almonds

1 teaspoon butter

2.5cm (1in) piece creamed coconut

200ml (7fl oz) single cream

15g (½oz) finely chopped fresh coriander leaves

salt

Heat the oil in a saucepan and fry the onion until light brown. Add the coriander-cumin powder, chilli powder, turmeric, ginger and garlic and fry over a high heat for 2 minutes, adding tablespoons of water to prevent the spices from sticking and burning. Add the tomato purée and continue to fry for about 3 minutes, adding further tablespoons of water. When you can see the oil begin to separate from the spices at the edges of the pan, add the vegetables and salt and sauté for 2-3 minutes. Next, add the ground almonds, butter and creamed coconut. As soon as the creamed coconut has melted, add the single cream and fresh coriander and let it simmer for 5 minutes before serving.

PUNJABI CHANA
Punjabi-style chickpeas

Punjab lies in the north of India and its cuisine is renowned for its hearty flavours. The area is known as the granary of India, and most Punjabi vegetable dishes are eaten with wholesome breads; *kulchas*, a thick fried bread, is the type most often served with this dish. The ginger aids the digestion of the chickpeas.

6 tablespoons oil

1 tablespoon cumin seeds

7.5cm (3in) piece ginger, cut into fine slivers

2 medium onions, peeled and finely sliced

1½ tablespoons coriander-cumin powder

1 teaspoon freshly ground black pepper

800g (1lb 12oz) tinned chickpeas

1 cup tea made with 4 tea bags (not herbal!)

½ teaspoon annar dana (pomegranate seeds; see Stockists)

2 tomatoes, chopped

½ teaspoon garam masala powder (see Stockists)

15g (½oz) finely chopped fresh coriander leaves

salt

Heat the oil in a saucepan and fry the cumin seeds together with the ginger and onions until the onions are soft and brown at the edges. Add the coriander-cumin powder, black pepper and chickpeas. Then add the tea and leave to simmer for 5 minutes. Next, add the *annar dana*, salt and tomatoes and leave to cook for 5 more minutes. Garnish with the *garam masala* powder and fresh coriander before serving.

STUFFED GREEN PEPPERS

Stuffed green peppers are as popular in India as they are in the West. This is a vegetarian recipe, but a stuffing of leftover mince with rice is a delicious variation.

4 medium potatoes, weighing about 750g (1lb 10oz)

6 tablespoons oil

1 small onion, peeled and finely chopped

1 teaspoon puréed garlic/5 cloves garlic, peeled and crushed

½ teaspoon chilli powder

25g (1oz) finely chopped fresh coriander leaves

4 green peppers

salt

First cook the potatoes in their skins in a pan of boiling salted water until tender. Drain, cool, peel and mash them. Set aside. Next, heat 4 tablespoons of the oil in a frying pan, then add the onion and fry until brown at the edges. Add the garlic, chilli powder, mashed potato, salt and half the fresh coriander. Set aside. Slice one end off each of the green peppers (the end with the stem) and set aside. Scoop out the seeds and stuff with the mash mixture. Top with the ends that have been set aside. Pour the remaining oil into a pan into which the peppers will fit snugly, add the peppers, cover and leave to cook over a low heat, until soft. Serve garnished with the remaining fresh coriander.

BAGARA BAIGAN
Spicy sautéed aubergine

In this dish from Hyderabad, aubergines are cooked with onions and spices, and finished off with a *tarka* of curry leaves and mustard seeds. Lemon juice adds zest.

> 8 tablespoons oil
> 2 medium aubergines (eggplants) halved, lengthways, without breaking the stems
> 3 large onions, peeled and finely sliced
> 1 teaspoon puréed garlic/5 cloves garlic, peeled and crushed
> ¼ teaspoon turmeric
> 4 teaspoons coriander-cumin powder
> ½ teaspoon chilli powder
> 2 green chillies, deseeded and finely chopped
> 1 teaspoon brown sugar
> 2 teaspoons lemon juice
> 2.5cm (1in) piece creamed coconut
> 5 curry leaves (preferably fresh)
> ½ teaspoon mustard seeds
> 15g (½oz) finely chopped fresh coriander leaves
> salt

Heat 6 tablespoons of the oil in a frying pan. Add the aubergines and cook until the skins turn light brown. Remove and set aside. In the same oil, fry the onions until soft. Add the garlic, turmeric, coriander-cumin powder, chilli powder and green chillies. Fry over a high heat for 5-7 minutes, adding tablespoons of water to prevent sticking and burning.

When you can see the oil begin to separate from the spices at the edges of the pan, return the aubergines to the pan along with 250ml (9fl oz) of water and cook over a low heat until the aubergines are tender.

Next, add salt, the brown sugar, lemon juice and creamed coconut. Let the creamed coconut dissolve, but do not overcook, as it tends to thicken and curdle. As soon as it has dissolved, remove the pan from the heat. Meanwhile, in a separate frying pan, heat the remaining oil. When it is very hot, drop in a curry leaf. If it sizzles and turns a darker shade, add all the other leaves and the mustard seeds. If the leaf turns very dark, reduce the heat and add the remaining curry leaves and mustard seeds after 1 minute. Pour this *tarka* over the aubergines, cover immediately and leave for 2 minutes, to allow the flavours to infuse. Garnish with the fresh coriander and serve.

DAHI KI CURRY
Yogurt curry

This curry is a boon to busy cooks everywhere, as it is very simple to make. I usually serve it with *bhuni khichri* (rice and lentil pilau), and sometimes I add a few plain pakoras, see below. I also enjoy it with *bhindi ki bhaji* (okra with onions).

> *250g (9oz) natural yogurt*
> *1 tablespoon gram flour (besan; see Stockists)*
> *¼ teaspoon turmeric*
> *¼ teaspoon chilli powder*
> *3 tablespoons oil*
> *5 curry leaves*
> *1 teaspoon black mustard seeds*
> *1 teaspoon puréed garlic/5 cloves garlic, peeled and crushed*
> *1 tablespoon hara masala (chilli and coriander paste; see page 31)*
> *15g (½oz) finely chopped fresh coriander leaves*
> *salt*

In a mixing bowl, combine the yogurt with the gram flour, turmeric, chilli powder and salt. Add 250ml (9fl oz) of water to this mixture and set aside. Heat the oil in a saucepan. When it is very hot, drop in a curry leaf. If it sizzles and turns a darker shade, add all the other leaves, the mustard seeds and garlic. If the leaf turns very dark, reduce the heat and add the remaining curry leaves, mustard seeds and garlic after 1 minute. Add the yogurt mixture to this and stir well. Then add the *hara masala*, bring to the boil and reduce to a low heat for 5 minutes. For a thinner sauce, add more water. To serve, garnish with the fresh coriander.

PAKORAS
Gram-flour dumplings

In the previous chapter I give recipes for various vegetable *bhajiyas* (fritters), and these dumplings are made from the batter used for the *bhajiyas*.

175g (6oz) gram flour (besan; see Stockists)
oil, for deep-frying
salt

Mix the gram flour and salt with 100ml (3½fl oz) of water to form a thick batter. Next, roll the mixture into 10 small balls about 5cm (2in) in diameter. Heat enough of the oil in a *karai* or wok-like pan to deep-fry the pakoras, and deep-fry them for 3-4 minutes.

M E A T

Succulent, tender meats paired with robust spices and subtle herbs – a cornucopia of dishes, fiery or mild, from the simple to the sophisticated.

A BASIC CURRY SAUCE

A wonderful base, this can be stored in the fridge for up to 7 days, or for up to one month in the freezer. It is a good idea to make a large quantity, then store it and use it in small amounts. Add it to a few tablespoons of oil, then sautée the meat you are using in it. Add 400ml (14fl oz) of water for a thick sauce, or 850ml (1½ pints) for a thinner one, simmer over a low heat and garnish with fresh coriander when ready.

5 tablespoons oil
4 medium onions, peeled and finely chopped
1½ tablespoons coriander-cumin powder
¼ teaspoon turmeric
½ teaspoon chilli powder
2 teaspoons puréed garlic/10 cloves garlic, peeled and crushed
2 teaspoons puréed ginger
1 tablespoon tomato purée
2 each of cardamom pods, cinnamon sticks, bay leaves and cloves
(whole garam masala)
salt

Heat the oil in a frying pan and fry the onions until golden brown. Add the coriander-cumin powder, turmeric, chilli powder, garlic and ginger, and fry over a high heat for 10 minutes, adding tablespoons of water to prevent the mixture from sticking and burning (this is the *bhunao* technique). Add the tomato purée and whole *garam masala* and continue to *bhunao* for 10-15 minutes, until you can see the oil begin to separate from the spices at the edges of the pan. Now add salt, and *bhunao* for another 10 minutes. The thickness of the sauce will depend on the total amount of water added – I tend to use a small amount (about 400ml/14fl oz), for a thicker sauce.

KHEEMA PAR ANDA
Savoury mince with baked eggs

Minced meat is not considered particularly sophisticated, but I find it lends itself to a variety of really simple recipes. This easy dish is a great favourite among both the Parsee and Khoja communities, who sometimes add fenugreek.

4 tablespoons oil
2 medium onions, peeled and finely chopped
450g (1lb) minced beef or lamb
1 teaspoon puréed garlic/5 cloves garlic, peeled and crushed

1 teaspoon puréed ginger

1½ tablespoons coriander-cumin powder

¼ teaspoon turmeric

½ teaspoon chilli powder

1 teaspoon tomato purée

4 eggs

15g (½oz) finely chopped fresh coriander leaves

salt

Preheat the oven to 200°C, 400°F, gas mark 6. Heat the oil in a large pan and fry the onions until golden brown. Add the mince along with the garlic, ginger, coriander-cumin powder, turmeric, chilli powder and tomato purée. Fry over a high heat for 10 minutes, adding tablespoons of water to prevent sticking and burning. Then add 200ml (7fl oz) of water and salt, and leave to cook until the mince is tender and the sauce is fairly dry. Next, transfer to an ovenproof baking dish and crack the eggs on top. Place in the oven for 15 minutes, until the eggs are cooked. Garnish with the fresh coriander.

SAG GOSHT
Spicy meat with spinach

A hearty dish, here fenugreek can be substituted for the spinach or added along with it. Best eaten with *parathas* or chapatis (flat breads), or naan bread.

450g (1lb) leg lamb, cut into cubes

8 tablespoons oil

2 medium onions, peeled and finely chopped

2 teaspoons puréed garlic/10 cloves garlic, peeled and crushed

2 teaspoons puréed ginger

2 tablespoons coriander-cumin powder

¼ teaspoon turmeric

½ teaspoon chilli powder

1 tablespoon tomato purée

2 each of cardamom pods, cinnamon sticks, bay leaves and cloves (whole garam masala)

450g (1lb) spinach (fresh or frozen), leaves left whole or chopped

¼ teaspoon garam masala powder (see Stockists)

15g (½oz) finely chopped fresh coriander leaves

salt

First boil the meat in 1 litre (1¾pints) of water until tender (about 50 minutes). Using a pressure cooker is ideal, as it reduces the cooking time to 15 minutes. If you do use one, proceed with caution. Meanwhile, heat the oil in a pan and fry the onions until golden brown. Add the garlic, ginger, coriander-cumin powder, turmeric, chilli powder, tomato purée and whole *garam masala*. Fry over a high heat for 10 minutes, adding tablespoons of water from time to time to prevent burning and sticking.

When you can see the oil begin to separate from the spices at the edges of the pan, add the lamb, 850ml (1½ pints) of the meat stock, salt and the spinach. Leave to cook over a low heat, uncovered, until the spinach is well blended. This is a fairly dry dish, but do add more water if you prefer more sauce. To serve, sprinkle over the *garam masala* powder and fresh coriander.

ROGAN JOSH
Spicy red lamb cooked with yogurt and saffron

Traditionally from Kashmir, *rogan josh* usually contains the rich red chillies for which that region is well-known. *Rogan* means 'fat' and *josh* means 'heat'; this is a robust dish. Here, the addition of shallots lends it a distinctive flavour. Best eaten with *parathas* (flat bread), pilau rice or dill pilau, whose colour contrasts well with the deep red of the sauce.

> *450g (1lb) leg lamb, cut into cubes*
> *1 teaspoon puréed ginger*
> *1 teaspoon puréed garlic/5 cloves garlic, peeled and crushed*
> *8 tablespoons oil*
> *2 large onions, peeled and finely chopped*
> *5 shallots, peeled and finely chopped*
> *1½ tablespoons coriander-cumin powder*
> *½ teaspoon chilli powder*
> *3 each of cardamom pods, cinnamon sticks, bay leaves and cloves (whole garam masala)*
> *2 tablespoons natural yogurt*
> *1 tablespoon tomato purée*
> *pinch saffron threads*
> *¼ teaspoon garam masala powder (see Stockists)*
> *15g (½oz) finely chopped fresh coriander leaves*
> *salt*

First boil the lamb with the ginger and garlic in 1 litre (1¾pints) of water until tender (about 50 minutes). Using a pressure cooker is ideal, as it reduces the cooking time to 15 minutes. If you do use one, proceed with caution. Meanwhile, heat the oil and fry the onions and shallots until they are a rich golden brown. Add the coriander-cumin powder, chilli powder, salt, whole *garam masala* and 1 tablespoon of the lamb stock and fry over a high heat for a minute or two. Next, add 1 tablespoon of the yogurt and continue to fry the mixture, adding the second tablespoon once the first one has been absorbed, stirring briskly to prevent curdling. Then add the tomato purée and 3 tablespoons of water and continue to fry over a high heat. When you can see the oil begin to separate from the spices at the edges of the pan (about 5 minutes), add the lamb, saffron and about 400ml (14fl oz) of water or lamb stock, and leave to cook over a low heat for 15 minutes, adding more water or lamb stock if it becomes very dry. To serve, garnish with the *garam masala* powder and fresh coriander.

KHEEMA MATTAR
Mince with peas

This homely dish was very popular when I was growing up, though we could only have it in winter, when peas were plentiful. Peas are still not available all year round in India, since the freezer facilities are very, very minimal. This makes an excellent meal when paired with pilau rice and *tarka* daal (lentils infused with garlic).

> 6 tablespoons oil
> 3 medium onions, peeled and finely chopped
> 450g (1lb) minced beef or lamb
> 1 tablespoon tomato purée
> 2 teaspoons puréed ginger
> 2 teaspoons puréed garlic/10 cloves garlic, peeled and crushed
> ¼ teaspoon turmeric
> ½ teaspoon chilli powder
> 1½ tablespoons coriander-cumin powder
> 2 medium potatoes, peeled and quartered
> 100g (3½oz) peas
> 15g (½oz) finely chopped fresh coriander leaves
> salt

Heat the oil in a pan and fry the onions until golden brown. Add the mince, tomato purée, ginger, garlic, salt and spices and fry for about 10 minutes over a high heat, adding tablespoons of water to prevent sticking and burning. When you can see the oil begin to separate from the spices at the edges of the pan, add the potatoes and 568ml (1 pint) of water, and leave to cook over a low heat until the potatoes are tender (about 20 minutes). Then add the peas and cook for a further 5 minutes. Garnish with the fresh coriander and serve.

CHAAP
Mince with chilli and coriander paste and lemon juice

Though mince is not a popular dinner-party food, this is a dish that goes down well every time. The secret is to use freshly ground coriander and cumin seeds, whizzed in a coffee grinder or crushed with a pestle and mortar, and freshly made *hara masala* (chilli and coriander paste). In India this is usually eaten with naan bread.

1 tablespoon coriander seeds and 1 tablespoon cumin seeds,
or 2 tablespoons coriander-cumin powder
6 tablespoons oil
450g (1lb) minced beef or lamb
2 teaspoons puréed ginger
2 teaspoons puréed garlic/10 cloves garlic, peeled and crushed
4 tablespoons hara masala (chilli and coriander paste; see page 31)
2 tablespoons lemon juice
¼ teaspoon garam masala powder (see Stockists)
15g (½oz) finely chopped fresh coriander leaves
salt

If making the coriander-cumin powder from scratch, briefly dry-roast the coriander and cumin seeds in a frying pan until they begin to release their aroma, then grind them in a coffee grinder or crush to a powder with a pestle and mortar. Set aside. Next, heat the oil in a pan and fry the mince for 3 minutes over a high heat. Add the ginger, garlic, salt and crushed coriander and cumin seeds or coriander-cumin powder, and fry for 15 minutes, adding tablespoons of water to prevent sticking and burning. Then add the *hara masala* along with 400ml (14fl oz) of water and continue to fry for another 10 minutes. Remove from the heat, add the lemon juice and garnish with the *garam masala* powder and fresh coriander.

GOSHT-E-MEHBOOB
Tender pieces of lamb in a rich, robust sauce

Meat for the beloved – this dish is dedicated to my husband, Mehboob. The reason he likes it so much is that it is rich and spicy, but not the sort of curry that burns your mouth. It tastes exquisite if it is properly *bhunaoed* (see page 28).

450g (1lb) leg lamb, cut into cubes
6 tablespoons oil
2 large onions, peeled and finely sliced

2 each of cardamom pods, cinnamon sticks, bay leaves and cloves (whole garam masala)

2 teaspoons puréed ginger

2 teaspoons puréed garlic/10 cloves garlic, peeled and crushed

1½ tablespoons coriander-cumin powder

¼ teaspoon turmeric

½ teaspoon chilli powder

1 tablespoon tomato purée

¼ teaspoon garam masala powder (see Stockists)

15g (½oz) finely chopped fresh coriander leaves

salt

First boil the meat in 1 litre (1¾pints) of water until tender (about 50 minutes). Using a pressure cooker is ideal, as it reduces the cooking time to 15 minutes. If you do use one, proceed with caution. Meanwhile, heat the oil in a pan and fry the onions until golden brown. Add the whole *garam masala*, ginger, garlic, coriander-cumin powder, turmeric, chilli powder, tomato purée and salt. Fry the spices for at least 15 minutes, adding table-spoons of water or lamb stock to prevent sticking and burning. When you can see the oil begin to separate from the spices at the edges of the pan, add the lamb and 850ml (1½ pints) of water or lamb stock (if a drier curry is preferred, adjust the quantity of water accordingly), and simmer over a very low heat for 10 minutes, until the lamb is very tender. To serve, garnish with the *garam masala* powder and fresh coriander.

TAWA GOSHT
Succulent leg of lamb cooked with spices in a *tawa*

This dish takes its name from the pan in which it is traditionally cooked – a *tawa*, which is a slightly concave heavy-bottomed griddle pan made of cast iron. The nearest equivalent would be a flat heavy-bottomed frying pan, though the following dish cooked in anything other than a *tawa* will simply taste like an ordinary curry. To find out where to get hold of one, *see Stockists*.

450g (1lb) leg lamb, cut into cubes

6 tablespoons oil

2 onions, peeled and sliced

1 teaspoon puréed ginger

1 teaspoon puréed garlic/5 cloves garlic, peeled and crushed

1½ tablespoons coriander-cumin powder

¼ teaspoon turmeric

½ teaspoon red chilli powder

2 fresh tomatoes, chopped

½ teaspoon tomato purée

2 green chillies, deseeded and chopped

¼ teaspoon garam masala powder (see Stockists)

15g (½oz) finely chopped fresh coriander leaves

salt

Boil the meat in 1 litre (1¾pints) of water until tender (about 50 minutes). Using a pressure cooker is ideal, as it reduces the cooking time to 15 minutes. If you do use one, proceed with caution. Meanwhile, heat a *tawa* and add the oil, then fry the onions over a high heat until golden brown. Add the ginger, garlic, coriander-cumin powder, turmeric and red chilli powder and fry for 5 minutes, adding tablespoons of water or lamb stock to prevent sticking and burning. When you can see the oil begin to separate from the spices at the edges of the pan, add the tomatoes, tomato purée, green chillies and salt and continue to fry for 10 minutes. Add the lamb and a little water (not too much, or it will spill over the sides of the *tawa*) and cook over a low heat for 10 more minutes. Serve straight from the *tawa*, garnished with the *garam masala* powder and fresh coriander.

LAMB PASANDA
Lamb in a mild, creamy sauce with almonds

Pasand means 'to like', and perhaps it has been used to name this creamy dish because it seems to have universal appeal. The *pasanda* I grew up with was quite different to this: rich reddish brown in colour, the meat was cut against the grain from the thigh or calf – much like an escalope – and it was served with flaky *parathas* (flat bread).

8 tablespoons oil

450g (1lb) leg lamb, cut into cubes

1 large onion, peeled and very finely grated or puréed

1 teaspoon puréed ginger

1 teaspoon puréed garlic/5 cloves garlic, peeled and crushed

4 teaspoons coriander-cumin powder

¼ teaspoon chilli powder

2 each of cardamom pods, cinnamon sticks, bay leaves and cloves (whole garam masala)

4 tablespoons natural yogurt

2 tablespoons ground almonds

150ml (5fl oz) single cream

1 tablespoon coarsely ground almonds or cashew nuts

¼ teaspoon garam masala powder (see Stockists)

15g (½oz) finely chopped fresh coriander leaves
salt

Heat the oil in a pan, brown the pieces of lamb and set aside. In the same oil fry the onion for a few minutes, then add the ginger, garlic, coriander-cumin powder, chilli powder, salt and whole *garam masala*. Fry for 10 minutes, adding tablespoons of water to prevent sticking and burning. Then add the yogurt, a tablespoon at a time, waiting for one tablespoon to be absorbed before adding the next, stirring briskly to prevent curdling. When you can see the oil begin to separate from the spices at the edges of the pan, add the lamb and 400ml (14fl oz) of water or lamb stock and leave to cook over a low heat for 40 minutes, until the lamb is very tender.

Check from time to time to make sure it is not drying out; you will probably need to top up the water a few times. Next, add the ground almonds and cook for a few more minutes. Add the cream and coarsely ground nuts, cook for 5 more minutes, then garnish with the *garam masala* powder and fresh coriander and serve.

METHI GOSHT
Spicy meat with fenugreek

The lamb here should be so tender it will literally melt in the mouth. If you are able to obtain fresh fenugreek, soak it for 20 minutes in salted water before using it to remove any bitterness. Frozen fenugreek is also very good. The world's best fenugreek comes from Qasur in Pakistan, which is why dried fenugreek powder is often referred to as *Kasoori methi* (*methi* means 'fenugreek'). Serve with *parathas* (flat bread) or naan bread.

450g (1lb) leg lamb, cut into cubes
2 teaspoons puréed garlic/10 cloves garlic, peeled and crushed
2 teaspoons puréed ginger
8 tablespoons oil
2 medium onions, peeled and finely chopped
1½ tablespoons coriander-cumin powder
2 teaspoons chilli powder
¼ teaspoon turmeric
1 tablespoon tomato purée
2 each of cardamom pods, cinnamon sticks, bay leaves and cloves (whole garam masala)
55g (2oz) chopped fenugreek leaves (preferably fresh) or spinach
¼ teaspoon garam masala powder (see Stockists)
15g (½oz) finely chopped fresh coriander leaves
salt

First boil the meat in 1 litre (1¾pints) of water with the garlic and ginger until tender (about 50 minutes). Using a pressure cooker is ideal, as it reduces the cooking time to 15 minutes. If you do use one, proceed with caution. Meanwhile, heat the oil in a pan and fry the onions until golden brown. Add the coriander-cumin powder, chilli powder, turmeric, salt, tomato purée and whole *garam masala*. Fry this mixture over a high heat for 10 minutes, adding tablespoons of lamb stock or water to prevent it from burning and sticking. When you can see the oil begin to separate from the spices at the edges of the pan, add the meat and 850ml (1½ pints) of stock or water, together with the spinach or fenugreek. Leave to cook over a low heat until the spinach or fenugreek is soft and the sauce is of the required consistency (drier or more liquid, whichever you prefer). To serve, sprinkle with the *garam masala* powder and fresh coriander.

AAB GOSHT
A classic, delicately flavoured lamb dish

Aab means 'water' in Persian, which explains the soupy consistency of this dish. This is good to serve to those who are sceptical about eating hot Indian food, as the flavours are subtle and fragrant rather than spicy. It is best served with plain white rice.

450g (1lb) leg lamb, cut into cubes
2 teaspoons puréed ginger
2 teaspoons puréed garlic/10 cloves garlic, peeled and crushed
2 tablespoons hara masala (coriander and chilli paste; see page 31)
6 tablespoons oil
2 medium onions, peeled and finely chopped
55g (2oz) chana daal (golden yellow lentils; see Stockists),
soaked for 2 hours
6 shallots, peeled and left whole
2 green chillies, deseeded and chopped
100g (3½oz) creamed coconut
1 teaspoon whole cumin seeds
1 tablespoon lemon juice
15g (½oz) finely chopped fresh coriander leaves
salt

First boil the meat, ginger, garlic, *hara masala* and salt in 1 litre (1¾pints) of water until tender (about 50 minutes). Using a pressure cooker is ideal, as it reduces the cooking time to 15 minutes. If you do use one, proceed with caution. Meanwhile, heat 5 tablespoons of the oil in a pan and fry the onions until translucent. Add the *chana* daal and 500ml (18fl oz) of water and cook until tender (about 20 minutes; the daals must still be whole but soft to the bite). Next, add the shallots, chillies and the lamb with the stock and cook for 10 minutes, until tender. Then add another 500ml (18fl oz) of water along with the creamed coconut and let it dissolve. Be careful, as it tends to curdle if over-cooked. Remove the pan from the heat as soon as it has melted. At this point, add more water if necessary – the dish should have a fairly soupy consistency. Meanwhile, heat the remaining tablespoon of oil. When it is very hot, add a couple of the cumin seeds. If they sizzle and turn a darker colour, add the rest. If the cumin seeds turn very dark, reduce the heat and add the rest after 1 minute. Immediately pour this *tarka* over the dish, followed by the lemon juice. To serve, garnish with the fresh coriander.

ACHAAR GOSHT
Lamb with pickle spices

The spices used to make this fairly dry dish are similar to those used in popular Indian pickles (*achaar* is the Indian word for pickles). To vary the dish, add chopped fenugreek or spinach leaves to it 10 minutes before the lamb is completely cooked. Best eaten with *parathas* or chapatis (flat breads), or naan bread.

> *450g (1lb) leg lamb, cut into cubes*
> *1 teaspoon fennel seeds*
> *1 teaspoon cumin seeds*
> *1 teaspoon mustard seeds*
> *1 teaspoon onion seeds*
> *½ teaspoon fenugreek seeds*
> *5 large green chillies*
> *6 tablespoons oil*
> *2 onions, peeled and finely chopped*
> *¼ teaspoon turmeric*
> *2 teaspoons puréed garlic/10 cloves garlic, peeled and crushed*
> *2 teaspoons puréed ginger*
> *5 tablespoons natural yogurt*
> *15g (½oz) finely chopped fresh coriander leaves*
> *salt*

First boil the meat in 1 litre (1¾pints) of water until tender (about 50 minutes). Using a pressure cooker is ideal, as it reduces the cooking time to 15 minutes. If you do use one, proceed with caution. Coarsely grind the fennel, cumin, mustard, onion and fenugreek seeds in a coffee grinder or with a pestle and mortar. Then slit each chilli down the middle and stuff with half the spice mixture, setting the rest aside. Heat the oil in a pan and fry the chillies for 2 minutes. Next, add the onions and fry until pale. Add the remaining spice mixture, turmeric, salt, ginger and garlic. Now add the yogurt a tablespoon at a time, stirring briskly to prevent curdling, waiting for 1 tablespoon to be absorbed before adding the next. Add all the yogurt in this way. Next add the lamb and half the fresh coriander and leave to cook for 10 minutes, until the lamb is tender and has absorbed the spices. Garnish with the remaining fresh coriander.

DAAL GOSHT
Spicy lentils with lamb

The basic idea for this dish is popular among both the Muslims and the Parsees. The Parsee version is called *dhansak*, a slightly more robust dish. *Dhansak* powder is made from fenugreek, cloves and black cardamom pods and is only available from Indian supermarkets. Usually eaten with caramelized brown rice and *cachumbar* (raw vegetable relish), this dish tastes even better the day after cooking. If you do make it a day ahead, the lentils will probably thicken the sauce. If this is the case, simply add about 200ml (7fl oz) of water to loosen the sauce, and bring to the boil before serving.

> *175g (6oz) mixed daals – chana (golden yellow lentils), toor (deep yellow lentils) and masoor (red lentils) (see Stockists)*
>
> *1 small aubergine (eggplant)*
>
> *½ teaspoon turmeric*
>
> *450g (1lb) leg lamb, cut into cubes*
>
> *2 teaspoons puréed ginger*
>
> *2 teaspoons puréed garlic/10 cloves garlic, peeled and crushed*
>
> *6 tablespoons oil*
>
> *2 onions, peeled and finely chopped*
>
> *1 teaspoon red chilli powder*
>
> *1½ tablespoons coriander-cumin powder*
>
> *2 each of cardamom pods, cinnamon sticks, bay leaves and cloves (whole garam masala)*
>
> *2 teaspoons dhansak powder (optional; see Stockists)*
>
> *1 tablespoon tomato purée*
>
> *2 green chillies, deseeded and chopped*
>
> *1 teaspoon lemon juice*
>
> *¼ teaspoon garam masala powder (see Stockists)*
>
> *15g (½oz) finely chopped fresh coriander leaves*
>
> *salt*

Soak the daals for at least 2 hours, or overnight, then boil them in a large pan with the aubergine, salt and a pinch of the turmeric in 3 litres (5¼ pints) of water until the mixture is very soft (about 40 minutes; 15 minutes in a pressure cooker), then whisk to the point where it reaches a soup-like consistency. Meanwhile, boil the lamb with the ginger and garlic in 1 litre (1¾ pints) of water until almost tender (about 50 minutes). Using a pressure cooker is ideal, as it reduces the cooking time to 15 minutes. If you do use one, proceed with caution. Set aside the lamb stock. While both the lamb and the lentils are cooking, heat the oil in a pan and fry the onions until golden brown. Add the red chilli powder, coriander-cumin powder, whole *garam masala*, *dhansak* powder (if using), remaining turmeric and salt, and fry for at least 10 minutes, adding tablespoons of water to prevent sticking and burning, until you can see the oil begin to separate from the spices at the edges of the pan. Now add the tomato purée and green chillies, followed by the lentils and the lamb, together with the lamb stock, and simmer for 20 minutes over a low heat. After this time, pour over the lemon juice, and garnish with the *garam masala* powder and fresh coriander before serving.

NARIYAL WALA GOSHT
Lamb with coconut milk and fresh coriander

A light green curry, this is mild and fresh. It has the sweetness of coconut, the tang of lemon and the fragrance of fresh coriander, and is delicious served with plain pilau rice.

> *450g (1lb) leg lamb, cut into cubes*
> *1 teaspoon puréed ginger*
> *1 teaspoon puréed garlic/5 cloves garlic, peeled and crushed*
> *4 tablespoons oil*
> *1 medium onion, peeled and finely chopped*
> *4 tablespoons hara masala (coriander and chilli paste, see page 31)*
> *3 bay leaves*
> *425ml (15fl oz) coconut milk*
> *2 tablespoons lemon juice*
> *15g (½oz) finely chopped fresh coriander leaves*
> *salt*

Boil the lamb in 1 litre (1¾ pints) of water with the ginger, garlic and salt until tender (about 50 minutes). Using a pressure cooker is ideal, as it reduces the cooking time to 15 minutes. If you do use one, proceed with caution. Set aside the lamb stock. Heat the oil in a pan and fry the onion until translucent. Then add the *hara masala*, bay leaves, coconut milk, salt and lamb. Leave to simmer over a low heat for about 15 minutes, topping it up from time to time with the stock to stop it from drying out. The consistency of the sauce should be that of unbeaten double cream. Remove from the heat, add the lemon juice and garnish with the fresh coriander before serving.

🌿 CHICKEN

Infused with fresh coriander; marinated and smothered in cream and coconut; fried in tongue-tingling spices – a range of subtle, rich and fragrant dishes.

MURGI KA SALNA
Simple, everyday chicken curry

This was the first curry I subjected my children to! They still enjoy it tremendously, and as they have grown up I have increased the quantities of chilli powder and coriander-cumin powder. It can be eaten with rice or chapatis (flat bread). The sauce should be thinner (simply add more water) if rice is the accompaniment.

> *6 tablespoons oil*
> *3 onions, peeled and finely chopped*
> *2 teaspoons puréed ginger*
> *2 teaspoons puréed garlic/10 cloves garlic, peeled and crushed*
> *¼ teaspoon chilli powder*
> *1½ tablespoons coriander-cumin powder*
> *½ teaspoon turmeric*
> *1 tablespoon tomato purée*
> *2 potatoes, peeled and quartered*
> *900g (2lb) chicken on the bone, divided into 8-10 small pieces*
> *15g (½oz) finely chopped fresh coriander leaves*
> *salt*

Heat the oil in a pan and fry the onions until golden brown. Add the ginger, garlic, chilli powder, coriander-cumin powder and turmeric and fry for about 10 minutes over a high heat, adding tablespoons of water from time to time to prevent the mixture from sticking and burning.

When you can see the oil begin to separate from the spices at the edges of the pan, add the tomato purée, potatoes, chicken and salt. Fry for a couple of minutes before adding 850ml (1½ pints) of water. Bring the mixture to the boil and leave it to simmer, uncovered, over a very low heat until the chicken and potatoes are cooked (about 30 minutes). Serve garnished with the fresh coriander.

CHICKEN TIKKA MASALA
Marinated smoked chicken in a rich, creamy sauce

In the UK, this is so popular it has come to be considered a national dish – despite its evident origins in Indian cuisine! Yet if you were to ask for this in India, no one would know what you were talking about, because although the components of this dish are Indian, the recipe is not.

You will find the recipe for the chicken *tikkas* on page 40 of this book; the recipe below is for the sauce. This is best eaten with naan bread.

chicken tikkas (see page 40)

3 tablespoons oil

1 large onion, peeled and very finely chopped

2 tablespoons tomato purée

pinch saffron threads

2 tablespoons ground almonds

300ml (10fl oz) single cream

1 tablespoon butter

pinch garam masala powder (see Stockists)

15g (½oz) finely chopped fresh coriander leaves

salt

Prepare the chicken *tikkas* according to the recipe on page 40. In a pan heat the oil and fry the onion until golden brown. Add the tomato purée, saffron, salt and about 2 tablespoons of water, followed immediately by the ground almonds, single cream and the chicken *tikkas* with all their juices. Bring to the boil and simmer for 5 minutes. Then add the butter and, once it has melted, stir, remove from the heat, and garnish with the *garam masala* powder and fresh coriander to serve.

ZAFRANI MURG
Chicken with saffron

A milder alternative to chicken korma (see later on in this chapter), this fragrant, creamy dish is cooked with saffron. Best eaten with *parathas* (flat bread) or naan bread.

5 tablespoons oil

900g (2lb) chicken on the bone, divided into 8-10 small pieces

3 tablespoons milk

pinch saffron threads

100g (3½oz) coconut milk powder, mixed with 425ml (15fl oz) warm water

200g (7oz) natural yogurt

2 medium onions, peeled, boiled and puréed

1 tablespoon ground almonds

½ teaspoon chilli powder

½ tablespoon turmeric

15g (½oz) finely chopped fresh coriander leaves

salt

Preheat the oven to 200°C, 400°F, gas mark 6. Heat the oil and fry the chicken pieces until light brown. Remove and set aside in a lidded ovenproof dish. Warm the milk and add the saffron to it. Set aside to allow it to infuse. Mix together the coconut milk, yogurt, puréed onions, salt, almonds, chilli powder and turmeric.

Pour this mixture on top of the chicken and place it in the oven, covered, for about 40 minutes (the chicken should be very tender). Remove it from the oven, pour over the saffron-infused milk, cover, and set aside for another 10 minutes. Sprinkle over the fresh coriander, to serve.

MURG DILKHUSH
Chicken with coconut milk, potatoes and saffron

Murg means 'chicken' and *dilkhush* means 'pleases your heart', which probably explains why this mild, comforting dish has almost universal appeal! Cook the chicken on the bone to achieve the best flavour.

> *4 tablespoons oil*
> *1 large onion, peeled and sliced*
> *900g (2lb) chicken on the bone, divided into 8-10 small pieces*
> *2 tomatoes, roughly chopped*
> *1 teaspoon puréed ginger*
> *1 teaspoon puréed garlic/5 cloves garlic, peeled and crushed*
> *2 green chillies, deseeded and chopped*
> *½ teaspoon chilli powder*
> *2 teaspoons coriander-cumin powder*
> *¼ teaspoon turmeric*
> *200g (7oz) natural yogurt*
> *pinch saffron threads*
> *300ml (10fl oz) coconut milk*
> *8 small new potatoes, cut in half*
> *15g (½oz) finely chopped fresh coriander leaves*
> *salt*

Preheat the oven to 200°C, 400°F, gas mark 6. Heat the oil in a pan and fry the onion until golden brown. Add the chicken pieces and tomatoes, ginger, garlic, green chillies, chilli powder, coriander-cumin powder, turmeric and salt.

Fry this mixture over a high heat, adding a little yogurt at a time, waiting for one lot to be absorbed before adding the next, stirring briskly to avoid curdling. Then, add the saffron and coconut milk.

Transfer to an ovenproof dish, together with the potatoes, and cook in the oven for about 40 minutes. Ensure the chicken and potatoes are well cooked before removing, then garnish with the fresh coriander and serve.

JEERA CHICKEN
Chicken with cumin

A chicken dish of fairly recent origin, and perfect for cumin lovers. This is a fairly dry dish, which can be cooked in a *karai* or other wok-like pan, and is best served with *parathas* or chapatis (flat breads), or naan.

> 125g (4½oz) natural yogurt
> 2 teaspoons puréed garlic/10 cloves garlic, peeled and crushed
> 2 teaspoons puréed ginger
> 1 tablespoon cumin powder
> 450g (1lb) boneless chicken or 1 small chicken, divided into 8-10 small pieces
> 1 piece charcoal
> 7 tablespoons oil
> 2 medium onions, peeled and finely chopped
> 3 teaspoons cumin seeds
> ¼ teaspoon turmeric
> 2 chopped tomatoes
> 2 green chillies, deseeded and finely chopped
> 15g (½oz) finely chopped fresh coriander leaves
> salt

Combine the yogurt, garlic, ginger and cumin powder in a mixing bowl. Place the chicken pieces in an ovenproof dish with a tightly fitting lid and pour over the marinade. Marinate for at least 45 minutes. Next, heat the piece of charcoal until it is red hot, place it in the middle of the marinated chicken and pour 2 tablespoons of the oil on top of the charcoal – it will begin to smoke. Quickly cover the dish with the lid or kitchen foil, to prevent the smoke escaping, and leave it for 15 minutes, until the smoke has permeated the chicken. Next, heat the remaining oil in a pan and fry the onions until golden brown. Add the cumin seeds, turmeric, tomatoes and salt, followed by the chicken, green chillies and 400ml (14fl oz) of water. Cook over a low heat until the chicken is tender (about 30 minutes). Serve garnished with the fresh coriander.

CHICKEN KORMA
Chicken in a mild, creamy sauce

An eternal favourite, this is a Mogul dish that is still immensely popular. Originally, kormas were red or white, and this is the white version (known as *safed* korma). Some cooks add turmeric (about half a teaspoon), which lends it a yellow hue. I have omitted turmeric here. Serve this with *parathas* or chapatis (flat breads), or naan bread.

1 large onion, peeled and roughly chopped

2 tablespoons desiccated coconut

1 teaspoon cumin seeds

1 teaspoon coriander seeds

4 cloves garlic, peeled

2.5cm (1in) fresh ginger, peeled

6 tablespoons oil

½ teaspoon chilli powder

1 teaspoon tomato purée

450g (1lb) boneless chicken, cut into cubes

250ml (9fl oz) single cream

1 tablespoon ground almonds

¼ teaspoon garam masala powder (see Stockists)

15g (½oz) finely chopped fresh coriander leaves

salt

In a food processor, blend the onion, dessicated coconut, cumin seeds, coriander seeds, garlic and ginger together, adding 100ml (3½fl oz) of water to form a smooth paste. Heat the oil in a pan and fry the puréed mixture over a high heat for a few minutes, until the oil separates from it.

Then add the chilli powder, salt and tomato purée, and keep frying for a further 5 minutes, adding tablespoons of water to prevent sticking and burning. Add the chicken and continue to fry for a few more minutes, then pour in 400ml (14fl oz) of water and leave to simmer until the chicken is tender (about 20 minutes). Now, reduce the heat to low, add the cream and almonds and cook for 5 more minutes. Serve sprinkled with the *garam masala* powder and the fresh coriander.

KARAI CHICKEN (1)
Chicken cooked in a karai with peppers and tomatoes

An easy, tasty dish, this takes its name from the utensil in which it is cooked. The technique required is similar to stir-frying, and if you don't possess a *karai*, any wok-like pan will do. Serve this with *parathas* or chapatis (flat breads), or naan bread.

5 tablespoons oil

450g (1lb) boneless chicken, cut into cubes

1 tablespoon puréed garlic/15 cloves garlic, peeled and crushed

1 teaspoon puréed ginger

400g (14oz) tinned chopped tomatoes

1 tablespoon coriander-cumin powder

½ teaspoon chilli powder

1 green chilli, deseeded and finely chopped

2 green peppers, deseeded and finely chopped

½ teaspoon fenugreek powder (Kasoori methi; see Stockists)

½ teaspoon garam masala powder (see Stockists)

15g (½oz) finely chopped fresh coriander leaves

salt

Heat the oil in a *karai* or wok-like pan, add the chicken and fry for a couple of minutes. Add the garlic and ginger and fry for 2 more minutes before adding the tomatoes, coriander-cumin powder, chilli powder, salt and the green chilli. Cook over a high heat until the chicken is tender (about 20 minutes), adding tablespoons of water to prevent sticking and burning. When you can see the oil begin to separate from the spices at the edges of the pan, add the peppers and fenugreek powder and leave to cook for 5 minutes. Sprinkle with the *garam masala* powder and serve garnished with the fresh coriander.

KARAI CHICKEN (2)

Another dish requiring the use of a *karai* or wok-like pan, serve this with *parathas* or chapatis (flat breads), or naan bread.

7 tablespoons oil

2 medium onions, peeled and finely chopped

1 tablespoon puréed garlic/15 cloves garlic, peeled and crushed

900g (2lb) chicken on the bone, divided into small pieces

400g (14oz) tinned chopped tomatoes

¼ teaspoon chilli powder

¼ teaspoon turmeric

2 sweet peppers, deseeded and cut into 5cm (2in) squares

¼ teaspoon cumin seeds

¼ teaspoon garam masala powder (see Stockists)

15g (½oz) finely chopped fresh coriander leaves

salt

Heat 4 tablespoons of the oil in a *karai* or wok-like pan and fry the onions until golden brown. Add the garlic and chicken and fry for a couple of minutes, then add the tomatoes and leave to cook over a low heat until the chicken is tender (about 30 minutes). Now add salt, the chilli powder and turmeric and fry over a very low heat, adding tablespoons of water to prevent sticking and burning. After about 5 minutes you should start to see the oil begin to separate from the spices at the edges of the pan.

Meanwhile, in a separate pan, heat 2 tablespoons of the remaining oil and fry the peppers for 2-3 minutes. Add them to the chicken. In a third pan (a small one), heat the remaining tablespoon of oil and, when it is very hot, add a couple of the cumin seeds. If they pop immediately and turn a darker colour, add the rest. If they turn a very dark colour, reduce the heat and add the remaining cumin seeds after 1 minute. Remove the pan from the heat immediately, pour this *tarka* over the chicken and serve garnished with the *garam masala* powder and fresh coriander.

DHANIA CHICKEN
Coriander chicken

A dry dish, best served with *parathas* or chapatis (flat breads), or naan bread.

> *½ teaspoon freshly ground black pepper*
> *2 teaspoons puréed garlic/10 cloves garlic, peeled and crushed*
> *½ teaspoon puréed ginger*
> *¼ teaspoon turmeric*
> *900g (2lb) chicken on the bone, divided into 8-10 small pieces*
> *8 tablespoons oil*
> *4 green chillies*
> *200g (7oz) tinned chopped tomatoes*
> *175g (6oz) finely chopped fresh coriander leaves*
> *salt*

Combine the salt, black pepper, garlic, ginger and turmeric in a bowl and leave the chicken to marinate in the mixture for at least 4 hours, or overnight. When you are ready to cook the chicken, heat the oil in a lidded frying pan and fry the chicken, a few pieces at a time, until crisp and brown. Set aside. Remove most of the excess oil from the pan, leaving approximately 1 tablespoon. Return all the chicken pieces to the pan, cover, place over a low heat, and cook for about 20 minutes, until tender. Then add the green chillies, tinned tomatoes and fresh coriander. Combine, reduce the heat to low, and cook for 10 minutes before serving.

CHICKEN JALFREZI
Spicy chicken with peppers and onions

> *8 tablespoons oil*
> *4 medium onions, peeled, 2 finely chopped*
> *and 2 coarsely chopped*

2 teaspoons puréed garlic/10 cloves garlic, peeled and crushed

1 teaspoon puréed ginger

1½ tablespoons coriander-cumin powder

½ teaspoon chilli powder

½ teaspoon turmeric

1 tablespoon tomato purée

5 tablespoons natural yogurt

450g (1lb) boneless chicken, cut into cubes

200g (7oz) tinned chopped tomatoes

3 green chillies, deseeded and coarsely chopped

2 peppers (1 green, 1 red), deseeded and chopped
into 5cm (2in) squares

pinch garam masala powder (see Stockists)

15g (½oz) finely chopped fresh coriander leaves

salt

Heat the oil in a pan and fry the finely chopped onions until brown at the edges. Add the coarsely chopped onions and fry for a further 5 minutes. Then add the garlic, ginger, coriander-cumin powder, chilli powder, turmeric and tomato purée. Now add the yogurt a tablespoon at a time, waiting for 1 tablespoon to be absorbed before adding the next, stirring briskly to prevent curdling. Then add the chicken and fry for 5 more minutes. Add the tomatoes and salt and fry for a further 2 minutes. Then add the green chillies and peppers, and leave to cook over a very low heat until the chicken is tender (about 20 minutes). To serve, sprinkle over the *garam masala* powder and fresh coriander.

CHICKEN DO PYAZA
Spicy chicken with onions

A popular dish, onions are the dominant flavour here. *Do* means 'two' and *pyaz* means 'onions'. Serve with chapatis (flat bread) or naan bread.

6 tablespoons oil, plus extra if needed

900g (2lb) chicken on the bone, divided into 8-10 small pieces

2 large onions, peeled, 1 sliced lengthways (from root to tip) and
1 finely chopped

6 shallots, peeled and coarsely chopped

1 tablespoon puréed garlic/15 cloves garlic, peeled and crushed

1 teaspoon puréed ginger

½ teaspoon turmeric

½ teaspoon chilli powder

2 tablespoons coriander-cumin powder

1 cardamom pod, cinnamon stick, bay leaf and clove (whole garam masala)

1 tablespoon tomato purée

5 tablespoons natural yogurt

pinch garam masala powder (see Stockists)

15g (½oz) finely chopped fresh coriander leaves

salt

Heat the oil in pan and fry the pieces of chicken for 3 minutes on each side. Remove and set aside. In the same oil, fry the onions you have sliced lengthways. Remove when light brown and drain on kitchen paper.

Now, adding more oil if needed, fry the finely chopped onions until golden brown. Then add the shallots, garlic, ginger, salt, turmeric, chilli powder, coriander-cumin powder and the whole *garam masala*. Fry over a high heat, adding tablespoons of water from time to time to prevent the mixture from sticking and burning.

When you can see the oil begin to separate from the spices at the edges of the pan, add the tomato purée and chicken, followed by the yogurt and 100ml (3½fl oz) of water. Leave to simmer until the chicken is tender (about 30 minutes). To serve, garnish with the fried sliced onions, *garam masala* powder and fresh coriander.

KUKU PAKA
Chicken with a sauce of creamy coconut, fresh coriander and lemon juice

A very popular dish, this comes from the East African Ismaili community. The name is Swahili and means 'chicken' (*kuku*) 'stew' (*paka*). Once it has been marinated, the chicken can be smoked using the *dhuan* technique (see page 28), which lends the dish a wonderful smoky flavour.

This is decorated with boiled eggs when served on special occasions. Serve with chapatis or *parathas* (flat breads), or naan bread.

5 tablespoons natural yogurt

2 teaspoons puréed garlic/10 cloves garlic, peeled and crushed

2 teaspoons puréed ginger

¼ teaspoon chilli powder

900g (2lb) chicken on the bone, divided into 8-10 small pieces

1 tablespoon hara masala (coriander and chilli paste, see page 31)

2 medium tomatoes, quartered

pinch turmeric

200g (7oz) creamed coconut

1 tablespoon lemon juice

15g (½oz) finely chopped fresh coriander leaves
salt

Combine the yogurt, garlic, ginger, chilli powder and salt in an ovenproof dish and marinate the chicken in this mixture for at least 45 minutes, or overnight. Once the chicken has marinated, it can be smoked using the *dhuan* technique (see page 28), which adds an extra-special flavour to the finished dish. (This is optional.) Preheat the oven to 200°C, 400°F, gas mark 6 and roast the chicken for 40 minutes. Then heat 850ml (1½ pints) of water in a pan and add the *hara masala*, tomatoes, turmeric and chicken. Bring to the boil, add the creamed coconut and let it melt. Do not overcook, as the creamed coconut tends to thicken and curdle. Remove the pan from the heat as soon as it has melted. If a thinner sauce is preferred, add more water at this point. To serve, add the lemon juice and garnish with remaining fresh coriander.

BALTI CHICKEN
Chicken with almonds, fenugreek and cream

The style of cooking known as *balti* cooking, taken from the name of a traditional Indian cooking pan, is enormously popular in the UK, even though it is unheard of in India. Serve with *parathas* (flat bread) or naan bread.

3 tablespoons natural yogurt
2 teaspoons puréed garlic/10 cloves garlic, peeled and crushed
2 teaspoons puréed ginger
2 teaspoons chicken tikka masala powder (see Stockists)
1 tablespoon lemon juice
450g (1lb) boneless chicken, cut into cubes
5 tablespoons oil
2 medium onions, peeled and finely chopped
1 tablespoon tomato purée
2 tablespoons chopped tomatoes
1 tablespoon coriander-cumin powder
½ teaspoon chilli powder
½ teaspoon turmeric
1 green pepper, deseeded and sliced
1 tablespoon dried fenugreek leaves
75ml (2½fl oz) single cream
1 tablespoon ground almonds
1 tablespoon butter
¼ teaspoon garam masala powder (see Stockists)

15g (½oz) finely chopped fresh coriander leaves
salt

Combine the yogurt, garlic, ginger, chicken *tikka masala* powder and lemon juice in a bowl and marinate the chicken in this mixture for at least 2 hours or overnight. When you are ready to cook the chicken, heat the oil in a pan and fry the onions until brown at the edges. Then add the tomato purée, chopped tomatoes, coriander-cumin powder, chilli powder and turmeric. Fry over a high heat for 5 minutes, adding tablespoons of water to prevent the spices from sticking and burning. After this time you should see the oil begin to separate from the spices at the edges of the pan. Add the chicken, along with the marinade, and cook for 5 minutes before adding the sliced green pepper, fenugreek and salt. Cook over a low heat until the chicken is tender (about 20 minutes), then add the cream, almonds and butter and cook for 5 more minutes. To serve, sprinkle with the *garam masala* powder and fresh coriander.

CHICKEN MADRAS
Hot, fiery, spicy chicken

Not one for the faint-hearted! The wonderful orangey-red colour of this dish comes from the tomatoes and chilli powder. Best eaten with pilau rice.

5 tablespoons oil

2 medium onions, peeled and very finely chopped
(preferably in a food processor)

1 teaspoon chilli powder

1½ tablespoons coriander-cumin powder

½ teaspoon turmeric

1 teaspoon puréed garlic/5 cloves garlic, peeled and crushed

1 teaspoon puréed ginger

2 tablespoons tomato purée

2 red chillies, deseeded and chopped

450g (1lb) boneless chicken, cut into cubes

15g (½oz) finely chopped fresh coriander leaves

salt

Heat the oil in a pan and fry the onions until light brown. Add the chilli powder, coriander-cumin powder, turmeric, garlic, ginger, tomato purée, salt and chopped red chillies. Add a tablespoon of water and fry over a high heat for 10 minutes, adding further tablespoons of water to prevent sticking and burning. When you can see the oil begin to separate from the spices at the edges of the pan, add the chicken and stir well.

Add 500ml (18fl oz) of water and bring to the boil. Immediately reduce the heat to low and leave to cook until the chicken is tender (about 20 minutes). Garnish with the fresh coriander.

CHICKEN WITH GREEN PEPPERS

Peppers add a wonderful flavour to this curry, which is best served with *parathas* or chapatis (flat breads), naan bread or pilau rice. To spice it up further, add a few chopped fresh green chillies.

6 tablespoons oil
450g (1lb) boneless chicken, cut into cubes
3 medium onions, peeled and finely chopped
1 teaspoon puréed ginger
1 teaspoon puréed garlic/5 cloves garlic, peeled and crushed
1½ tablespoons coriander-cumin powder
¼ teaspoon turmeric
¼ teaspoon red chilli powder
1 tablespoon tomato purée
2 green peppers, deseeded and chopped into small squares
¼ teaspoon garam masala powder (see Stockists)
15g (½oz) finely chopped fresh coriander leaves
salt

Heat the oil in a pan and fry the chicken until the pieces are light brown. Remove the chicken and set aside. In the same oil, fry the onions until golden brown. Add the ginger, garlic, coriander-cumin powder, turmeric and chilli powder. Add a tablespoon of water and fry over a high heat, adding further tablespoons of water to prevent sticking and burning. When you can see the oil begin to separate from the spices at the edges of the pan, add the tomato purée and salt and continue fry over a high heat for another 5 minutes, adding a few more tablespoons of water. Add the chicken and 400ml (14fl oz) of water and leave to simmer until the chicken is tender (about 20 minutes), topping up the water if the sauce starts to dry out. When the chicken is ready, add the peppers and cook for a few minutes until they are tender. To serve, garnish with the *garam masala* powder and fresh coriander.

FISH AND SEAFOOD

Sweet and sour prawns; fish marinated in lemon juice, seasoned with chillies and simmered with creamed coconut... Simple dishes, magical results.

FRIED FISH WITH POTATOES

Fish cooked in an assortment of spices is popular all over India, and every community has its own special blend of spices. This version is the one I enjoy most, and is best served with chapatis (flat bread), though it also works very well with *tarka* daal (lentils infused with garlic) and rice. You can use any variety of fish you like; I tend to use cod.

900g (2lb) cod fillets, cut into 8 pieces
1 tablespoon lemon juice
3 tablespoons coriander-cumin powder
½ teaspoon turmeric
1 teaspoon chilli powder
8 tablespoons oil
4 medium potatoes, peeled, each one cut into 6 slices
2 medium onions, peeled and finely chopped
1 tablespoon puréed ginger
1 tablespoon puréed garlic/15 cloves garlic, peeled and crushed
2 tablespoons tomato purée
15g (½oz) finely chopped fresh coriander leaves
lemon wedges, to garnish
salt

In a glass dish, marinate the fish in a mixture of the lemon juice, 1 teaspoon of salt, 2 tablespoons of the coriander-cumin powder, the turmeric and chilli powder for 1 hour. After this time, heat the oil in a large frying pan and fry the potato slices over a low heat until almost done. Set aside. In the same oil, fry the fish for 2 minutes over a high heat. Set aside. Fry the chopped onions in the same oil until brown at the edges. Add the ginger, garlic, tomato purée and remaining coriander-cumin powder to the pan. Next, add a tablespoon of water and fry the mixture for a few minutes over a high heat, adding further tablespoons of water to prevent sticking and burning. When you can see the oil begin to separate from the spices, add the fish and potatoes together with 250ml (9fl oz) of water. Then leave to cook over a low heat, until the fish and potatoes are cooked through and have absorbed the spices (about 10 minutes). Garnish with the fresh coriander and wedges of lemon.

MACHI KA SALNA
Spicy fish curry

Pungent and spicy, the wonderfully vibrant bright orange colour of this delicious, easy dish comes from a combination of chillies and tomatoes. You can use any fish you like;

my particular favourites are cod and haddock. This takes very little time to assemble and cook, and is great with *bhuni khichri* (rice and lentil pilau).

> *2 tablespoons lemon juice*
> *2 teaspoons red chilli powder*
> *450g (1lb) fish cut into pieces measuring about 5 ₅ 10cm (2 ₅ 4in)*
> *½ teaspoon turmeric*
> *1½ tablespoons coriander-cumin powder*
> *1 tablespoon tomato purée*
> *6 tablespoons oil*
> *6 fresh curry leaves*
> *½ teaspoon black mustard seeds*
> *2 teaspoons puréed garlic/10 cloves garlic, peeled and chopped*
> *2 green chillies, left whole but slit down the middle*
> *l00g (3½oz) creamed coconut*
> *15g (½oz) finely chopped fresh coriander leaves*
> *salt*

Combine 1 teaspoon of salt, 1 tablespoon of the lemon juice and 1 teaspoon of the chilli powder and marinate the fish in this mixture for 30 minutes. Then, in a bowl, mix together the turmeric, coriander-cumin powder, the remaining teaspoon of chilli powder, the tomato purée and 125ml (4fl oz) of water. (This is the *masala* mixture.) Heat the oil in a large frying pan and, when it is very hot, drop in a curry leaf. If it sizzles and turns a darker shade, add all the other leaves and the mustard seeds. If it turns very dark, reduce the heat and wait for 1 minute before adding the remaining curry leaves and mustard seeds. Next, add the garlic and fry for 1 minute before adding the *masala* mixture. Stir briskly over a high heat. Then add the green chillies and 700ml (1¼ pints) of water. Bring to the boil. Add the fish and let it cook for 2 minutes before adding the creamed coconut. Let the creamed coconut dissolve over a low heat. This won't take long so be careful, as it tends to curdle if overcooked. As soon as it has melted, remove the pan from the heat. At this point, add more water if you want a thinner sauce. Finally, add the remaining lemon juice, and serve garnished with the fresh coriander.

PRAWN PATIA
Sweet and sour prawn curry

A popular Parsee recipe, the addition of tomato ketchup is not as unauthentic as it may appear; the ingredient traditionally used is jaggery (*gur*), a coarse brown sugar similar to molasses, but tomato ketchup produces the same result and is very convenient. Serve this with *bhuni khichri* (rice and lentil pilau), plain pilau rice or chapatis (flat bread).

8 cloves garlic, peeled

6 dried red chillies

2 teaspoons cumin seeds

450g (1lb) prawns (shrimps)

2 tablespoons lemon juice

5 tablespoons oil

5 medium onions, peeled and grated

1 tablespoon vinegar

¼ teaspoon sugar

2 tablespoons tomato ketchup

15g (½oz) finely chopped fresh coriander leaves

salt

In a coffee grinder or with a pestle and mortar, grind together the garlic cloves, dried red chillies and cumin seeds. Set aside. In a glass dish, marinate the prawns in the lemon juice and half a teaspoon of salt for 1 hour. In a pan, heat the oil, and fry the onions until golden brown. Add the ground-spice-and-garlic mixture and fry well for 2 minutes. Then add the prawns together with 250ml (9fl oz) of water and leave to simmer until cooked. Next, add the vinegar, sugar and tomato ketchup and simmer for 5 minutes. Serve garnished with the fresh coriander.

MASALA PRAWNS AND POTATOES
Spicy prawns and potatoes

This dish is wonderful served with hot chapatis (flat bread).

½ teaspoon lemon juice

450g (1lb) prawns (shrimps)

5 tablespoons oil

2 onions, peeled and finely chopped

1 tablespoon puréed garlic/15 cloves garlic, peeled and crushed

1 tablespoon puréed ginger

1 green chilli, deseeded and chopped

½ teaspoon turmeric

3 tablespoons coriander-cumin powder

½ teaspoon chilli powder

2 potatoes, peeled and diced

1 tablespoon tomato purée

15g (½oz) finely chopped fresh coriander leaves

salt

Combine the lemon juice with a pinch of salt and marinate the prawns in this mixture for 1 hour. Heat the oil in a large frying pan, add the onions and fry until golden brown. Add the garlic, ginger, green chilli, turmeric, coriander-cumin powder, chilli powder and a tablespoon of water and fry for 5 minutes, adding further tablespoons of water to prevent sticking and burning.

Then add the potatoes, tomato purée, salt and 250ml (9fl oz) of water, and leave to cook until the potatoes are tender (10-12 minutes). At this point, add the prawns and simmer for 5 minutes. It is important not to overcook the prawns, as they tend to get leathery. Garnish with the fresh coriander and serve immediately.

AMRITSARI FISH
Fried fish

This is a Punjabi recipe. Ajowan (sometimes referred to as carom), a spice commonly used in Indian cooking, is said to taste of a combination of anise and oregano with a hint of black pepper, and here it lends the dish an interesting flavour. These also taste wonderful when cooked on a barbecue instead of fried.

2 tablespoons puréed ginger
2 teaspoons puréed garlic/10 cloves garlic, peeled and crushed
1 tablespoon deseeded and finely chopped green chillies
2 tablespoons ajowan (carom) seeds (see Stockists)
2 eggs
pinch powdered orange food colouring dissolved in 1 teaspoon warm water or 1 teaspoon liquid orange food colouring
900g (2lb) cod steaks, cut into pieces measuring about 5 ₅ 10cm (2 ₅ 4in)
oil, for shallow-frying
15g (½oz) finely chopped fresh coriander leaves
¼ teaspoon garam masala powder (see Stockists)
lemon wedges
salt

In a coffee grinder or with a pestle and mortar, grind together the ginger, garlic, green chillies and ajowan seeds. Add 4 tablespoons of water to form a fine paste. Strain this mixture and retain the liquid, discarding the residue. Beat the eggs, adding salt and the liquid from the paste, together with the orange food colouring. Coat the fish in this marinade and leave for 40 minutes. After this time, heat enough of the oil in a frying pan to shallow-fry the fish. Fry until slightly speckled brown. Serve immediately, garnished with the fresh coriander, *garam masala* powder and the wedges of lemon.

 R I C E

From fragrant pilaus to exotic biryanis, the aroma of rice is hard to resist. Infused with saffron, sautéed with cumin or slow-cooked with lamb, the results are always unique.

Uncover a pan of perfectly cooked rice and the steam will waft towards you, enveloping your senses in a warm, fragrant haze. It is one of those great cooking experiences, something that, though repeated on a daily basis, always brings with it a sense of achievement and comfort.

Rice is the staple food of nearly half of India, and it is particularly popular among Bengalis and the communities in southern India. Easy to digest, it is one of the first solids given to babies, and is often administered to those convalescing after an illness. Rice forms the basis of simple pilaus (delicately flavoured rice dishes) to accompany everyday curries or to be eaten on their own, and it can be infused with rich spices and cooked with meat to make exotic biryanis, often the centrepieces of Indian wedding banquets.

Traditionally, biryani was the name given to the dish in which the meat or vegetables were placed at the bottom of the cooking vessel, and the rice on top. This was then cooked using the *dum* method (cooking the dish in its own steam) and served 'upside down' (the rice laid out on the base of the serving plate and the meat or vegetables spooned on top). Some of the more elaborate pilaus, which also involve combinations of rice and meat or vegetables cooked together using the *dum* technique, could be confused with biryanis. However, they are not layered in the same way, and this is the distinction between the two. *Masoor* pilau (rice, mince and lentil pilau), in which this layering does occur, is sometimes also referred to as a biryani.

Other uses for rice include grinding it into flour, and using it to make bread, *dosas* (crepes) or *idlis* (rice-flour cakes), popular dishes in southern India. It can also be flavoured with saffron and cardamom pods to create delicious *kheer* (rice pudding).

There are many varieties of rice, but basmati (which has a long grain that lengthens when cooked) is probably the most famous. My own experience is that it makes the perfect pilau every time, and I would recommend using it for all rice dishes. In India, people tend to use basmati only on special occasions, as it is more expensive than other varieties. Unlike spices, which should be as fresh as possible, year-old rice is considered the finest, and is more expensive in India. In the West, prepacked rice makes it difficult to gauge how old it is, though it can certainly be bought and stored (in a cool dry place) for far longer than spices.

There is no great mystery to making perfect rice. Buy the best-quality rice you can afford, measure it according to the recipe you are following and soak it for 30 minutes, then wash it thoroughly until the water runs clear (this gets rid of the starch, which is what makes rice sticky). Next, boil the rice in salted water. The general rule is to use 400ml (14fl oz) of water to 225g (8oz) of rice. Once the water begins to boil, the heat should be reduced to very low and the pan covered with a tightly fitting lid. The rice should then be cooked for 10 minutes in this way, without being uncovered. If you do remove the lid the steam necessary to cook the rice will escape, which will result in rice that is not evenly cooked. When cooking rice it is important to be gentle when moving the grains around, as they break quite easily, releasing starch.

PILAU RICE

Simplicity itself, the fragrance of whole *garam masala* adds a wonderful flavour to this classic side dish. Speckled with orange food colouring – and saffron threads, if you're feeling extravagant – pilau rice goes wonderfully well with almost any curry. The invention of the microwave means you can reheat any leftover rice to perfection.

> *225g (8oz) basmati rice*
> *2 tablespoons oil*
> *2 each of cardamom pods, cinnamon sticks, bay leaves and cloves (whole garam masala)*
> *pinch powdered orange food colouring dissolved in 1 teaspoon warm water or 1 teaspoon liquid orange food colouring*
> *pinch saffron threads soaked in 1 tablespoon hot water (optional)*
> *salt*

In a large bowl, soak the rice for 30 minutes, then rinse it until the water runs clear and loses its chalkiness. Next, in a saucepan with a tightly fitting lid, heat the oil to very hot. In order to ensure the oil is hot enough, drop in a clove or cardamom pod from the whole *garam masala*. If it sizzles and splutters at once, add the remaining spices from the whole *garam masala*. If it turns very dark, reduce the heat and add the remaining spices after 1 minute. Then, add the rice, stir gently and add salt and 400ml (14fl oz) of water. Bring to the boil. The minute it begins to boil, cover with the tightly fitting lid, reduce the heat to very low and leave to cook, without uncovering, for 10 minutes. After this time, remove the pan from the heat and set aside for another 5 minutes before uncovering. Next, sprinkle with the orange food colouring and saffron-infused water (if using) and use a fork to fluff up the rice gently before serving.

DILL PILAU

Delicious, aromatic and subtle, this looks stunning served with *gosht-e-Mehboob* (tender pieces of lamb in a rich, robust sauce), which is red in colour.

> *225g (8oz) basmati rice*
> *2 tablespoons oil*
> *1 small onion, peeled and finely chopped*
> *2 each of cardamom pods, cinnamon sticks, bay leaves and cloves (whole garam masala)*
> *25g (1oz) fresh dill, fronds only, finely chopped*
> *salt*

In a large bowl, soak the rice for 30 minutes, then rinse it until the water runs clear and loses its chalkiness. In a saucepan with a tightly fitting lid, heat the oil and fry the onion until brown at the edges. Next, add the whole *garam masala* and the dill and sauté for 1 minute. Then add the rice, stir, add salt and 400ml (14fl oz) of water. Bring to the boil. The minute it begins to boil, cover with the tightly fitting lid, reduce the heat to very low and leave to cook, without uncovering, for 10 minutes. After this time, remove the pan from the heat and set aside for another 5 minutes before uncovering. Use a fork to fluff up the rice gently before serving.

VEGETABLE PILAU

The addition of vegetables adds a different dimension to pilau rice – simple, colourful and tasty.

> 225g (8oz) basmati rice
> 3 tablespoons oil
> 1 medium onion, peeled and finely chopped
> 175g (6oz) mixed vegetables (fresh or frozen, including green peppers), chopped
> 2 each of cardamom pods, cinnamon sticks, bay leaves and cloves (whole garam masala)
> ½ teaspoon puréed garlic/2-3 cloves garlic, peeled and crushed
> ¼ teaspoon turmeric
> 1 green chilli, deseeded and finely chopped
> salt

In a large bowl, soak the rice for 30 minutes, then rinse it until the water runs clear and loses its chalkiness. In a saucepan with a tightly fitting lid, heat the oil and fry the onions until brown at the edges. Next add the vegetables, whole *garam masala*, garlic, turmeric, green chilli and salt. Add the rice, stir gently, then add 400ml (14fl oz) of water. Bring it to the boil. The minute it begins to boil, cover with the tightly fitting lid, reduce the heat to very low and leave to cook, without uncovering, for 10 minutes. After this time, remove the pan from the heat and set aside for another 5 minutes before uncovering. Use a fork to fluff up the rice gently before serving.

BROWN RICE

In the West, brown rice tends to refer to wholegrain rice, but here it describes the colour of the dish, imparted thanks to caramelized sugar and browned onions. The rice here has a lovely, rich flavour, but is not sweet, as the addition of sugar might lead one to expect (the can also be made without sugar). Traditionally, this is served with daal *gosht* (spicy lentils with lamb).

> *225g (8oz) basmati rice*
> *4 tablespoons oil*
> *2 medium onions, peeled and finely chopped*
> *2 each of cardamom pods, cinnamon sticks, bay leaves and cloves*
> *(whole garam masala)*
> *1 teaspoon sugar*
> *salt*

In a large bowl, soak the rice for 30 minutes, then rinse it until the water runs clear and loses its chalkiness. In a pan with a tightly fitting lid, heat the oil and fry the onions until golden brown. Add the whole *garam masala* and salt. Add the sugar and let it caramelize over a medium heat; this will take about 5 minutes, after which time it should be a rich brown colour. Add the rice, stir gently and add 400ml (14fl oz) of water. Bring to the boil. The minute it begins to boil, cover with the tightly fitting lid, reduce the heat to very low and leave to cook, without uncovering, for 10 minutes. After this time, remove the pan from the heat and set aside for another 5 minutes before uncovering. Use a fork to fluff up the rice gently before serving.

JEERA PILAU
Cumin pilau

Roasted cumin seeds sautéed with the rice add a wonderfully fragrant aroma to this dish. It goes well with all types of curries.

> *225g (8oz) basmati rice*
> *3 tablespoons oil*
> *2 teaspoons whole cumin seeds (dry-roasted in a frying pan for a couple*
> *of minutes, if desired)*
> *2 each of cardamom pods, cinnamon sticks, bay leaves and cloves*
> *(whole garam masala)*
> *salt*

In a large bowl, soak the rice for 30 minutes, then rinse it until the water runs clear and loses its chalkiness. Next, in a saucepan with a tightly fitting lid, heat the oil to very hot. In order to ensure the oil is hot enough, drop in a couple of cumin seeds. If they turn a darker colour and sizzle and splutter at once, add the remaining cumin seeds. If they turn very dark, reduce the heat and add the remaining cumin seeds after 1 minute. Then add the whole *garam masala*, followed by the rice. Stir gently, add salt and 400ml (14fl oz) of water and bring to the boil. The minute it begins to boil, cover with the tightly fitting lid, reduce the heat to very low and leave to cook, without uncovering, for 10 minutes. After this time, remove the pan from the heat and set aside for another 5 minutes before uncovering. Use a fork to fluff up the rice gently before serving.

FISH PILAU

My brother lives in Washington and this is one of his favourite dishes. I only make it when he visits, though must admit I love it, too. I also love cooking for my brother, as he really appreciates whatever I make him, and, like any cook, I adore anyone who enjoys my food! This is an unusual version of pilau rice, and the meltingly soft potatoes make a scrumptious addition. Serve with *cachumbar* (raw vegetable relish) or raita.

> *450g (1lb) basmati rice*
> *2 tablespoons lemon juice*
> *½ teaspoon chilli powder*
> *450g (1lb) fish fillets (eg cod or halibut)*
> *8 tablespoons oil*
> *4 medium potatoes, peeled and quartered*
> *2 onions, peeled and finely chopped*
> *2 tablespoons coriander-cumin powder*
> *½ teaspoon turmeric*
> *1 teaspoon puréed garlic/5 cloves garlic, peeled and crushed*
> *1 teaspoon puréed ginger*
> *1 tablespoon tomato purée*
> *2 each of cardamom pods, cinnamon sticks, bay leaves and cloves (whole garam masala)*
> *15g (½oz) finely chopped fresh coriander leaves*
> *¼ teaspoon garam masala powder (see Stockists)*
> *salt*

In a large bowl, soak the rice for 30 minutes, then rinse it until the water runs clear and loses its chalkiness. While the rice is soaking, combine half a teaspoon of salt, the lemon juice and a quarter teaspoon of the chilli powder in a mixing bowl and marinate the fish in this mixture for 30 minutes. Then, in a frying pan, heat 3 tablespoons of the oil and shallow-fry the fish until it turns light brown in colour. Remove and set aside. In the same oil, lightly fry the potatoes and set aside. In a pan (one that will fit into your oven) with a tightly fitting lid, heat the remaining oil and fry the onions until light brown.

Add the coriander-cumin powder, turmeric, remaining chilli powder, garlic, ginger, and tomato purée. Fry for a couple of minutes over a high heat with 1 tablespoon of water. Then add the whole *garam masala* and the rice and stir very gently to ensure the rice grains don't start to break up. Add 850ml (1½ pints) of water and 1 teaspoon of salt, then place the fish, potatoes and fresh coriander on top. Bring to the boil. The minute it begins to boil, cover with the lid, reduce the heat to very low and leave to cook, without uncovering, for 15 minutes. Preheat the oven to 150°C, 300°F, gas mark 2. Place the pan, still covered, in the oven and leave it for 20 minutes, after which time the potatoes should be well cooked and soft. Garnish with the *garam masala* powder and serve.

GOSHT PILAU (akni)
Lamb and potato pilau

My family and I belong to the Ismaili community (Muslims who regard the Aga Khan as their spiritual leader). Ismailis have settled all over the world, and this dish is typical of those who left India and have, since the early Seventies, settled in Europe and North America. This is often served at lunch parties instead of biryani, which is far richer and heavier to digest. The potatoes, which should be really soft, are most people's favourite element of this dish, and they often disappear before the pieces of lamb. Mild and delicious, it should be eaten with *cachumbar* (raw vegetable relish) or cucumber raita.

> *450g (1lb) basmati rice*
> *450g (1lb) leg lamb, cut into cubes*
> *2 tomatoes, quartered*
> *2 teaspoons puréed garlic/10 cloves garlic, peeled and crushed*
> *2 teaspoons puréed ginger*
> *2 tablespoons hara masala (chilli and coriander paste; see page 31)*
> *6 tablespoons oil*
> *2 medium potatoes, peeled and quartered (new potatoes also work very well with this dish)*
> *2 medium onions, peeled and finely chopped*
> *1 teaspoon cumin seeds, dry-roasted in a frying pan for a couple of minutes*
> *2 each of cardamom pods, cinnamon sticks, bay leaves and cloves (whole garam masala)*
> *salt*

In a large bowl, soak the rice for 30 minutes, then rinse it until the water runs clear and loses its chalkiness. Meanwhile, boil the lamb in 1 litre (1¾pints) of water with the tomatoes, garlic, ginger, *hara masala* and salt until the lamb is tender (about 50 minutes). Using a pressure cooker is ideal, as it reduces the cooking time to 15 minutes.

If you do use one, proceed with caution. In a pan (one that will fit into your oven) with a tightly fitting lid, heat the oil and fry the potatoes for 2 minutes, until pale brown. Remove and set aside. In the same oil, fry the onions until light brown, then add the cumin seeds and whole *garam masala*. Next, add the rice and stir gently. Add the potatoes and lamb together with 850ml (1½ pints) of water. Using the lamb stock is ideal, however if it isn't enough, add water to make up the full amount. Bring to the boil. The minute it begins to boil, cover with the tightly fitting lid, reduce the heat to very low and leave to cook, without uncovering, for 15 minutes. Preheat the oven to 150°C, 300°F, gas mark 2. Place the pan, still covered, in the oven and leave for 30 minutes. Then remove from the oven and set aside, still covered, for 5 minutes. The potatoes should be well done. Serve immediately; however, if it is to be eaten a bit later, keep in an oven preheated to 150°C, 300°F, gas mark 2 until ready to serve.

MASOOR PILAU
Rice, mince and lentil pilau

This rich dish, made with mince and lentils and delicately flavoured with saffron and spices, can be turned into a vegetarian dish simply by omitting the mince from the recipe. Best served with *cachumbar* (raw vegetable relish) or cucumber raita. On special occasions, this can be garnished with hard-boiled eggs, browned onions and fried cashew nuts.

225g (8oz) masoor daal (whole brown lentils), skins left on (see Stockists)

450g (1lb) basmati rice

4 medium potatoes, peeled and left whole

10 tablespoons oil

3 large onions, peeled and finely chopped

450g (1lb) minced beef or lamb

1 tablespoon puréed ginger

1 tablespoon puréed garlic/15 cloves garlic, peeled and crushed

3 tablespoons coriander-cumin powder

½ teaspoon turmeric

1 teaspoon chilli powder

1 tablespoon tomato purée

4 each of cardamom pods, cinnamon sticks, bay leaves and cloves (whole garam masala)

¼ teaspoon garam masala powder (see Stockists)

pinch saffron threads

pinch powdered orange food colouring dissolved in 1 teaspoon warm water or 1 teaspoon liquid orange food colouring

50ml (2fl oz) milk
salt

Soak the daal for at least 2 hours or overnight. In a large bowl, soak the rice for 30 minutes, then rinse it until the water runs clear and loses its chalkiness. Parboil the potatoes in their skins in a pan of boiling salted water for 5 minutes. Drain, cool and peel them. Set aside. In a saucepan, heat 8 tablespoons of the oil, fry the potatoes, whole, over a high heat for 2-3 minutes, until speckled brown, then set aside. Preheat the oven to 200°C, 400°F, gas mark 6. In the same oil, fry the onions until golden brown. Then add the mince, ginger, garlic, coriander-cumin powder, turmeric and chilli powder together with the tomato purée and half the whole *garam masala*. Add a little water and fry the mixture well over a high heat, adding a little more water from time to time to prolong the frying and stop the spices from sticking and burning, until you can see the oil begin to separate from the spices at the edges of the pan. At this point, add salt and the daal. Stir well, add 250ml (9fl oz) of water and continue to cook, adding more water if the mixture becomes very dry. The daal should be tender but remain whole, and the mixture should be dry. When it is ready, transfer to an ovenproof dish with a tightly fitting lid, sprinkle the *garam masala* powder on top and set aside. Now fill a pan with plenty of water and bring to the boil. Add salt, the remaining whole *garam masala* and the rice, and cook until the rice is parboiled (about 5 minutes – the grains should be partly cooked). Drain the rice and arrange it on top of the meat and daal. Now, in a small bowl, add the saffron to 1 tablespoon of boiling water. Next, scatter both the saffron-infused water and the orange food colouring on top of the rice mixture and make small holes in the rice. Pour the remaining oil and the milk into these openings. Cover tightly and place in the oven for 20 minutes. Then reduce the heat to 150°C, 300°F, gas mark 2 and leave for a further 30 minutes. Serve immediately.

BHUNI KHICHRI
Rice and lentil pilau

Usually eaten with spicy fish curry or *dahi ki curry* (yogurt curry), leftover *bhuni khichri* can be sautéed with onions, fresh coriander and green chillies to produce a variation of kedgeree (a popular Anglo-Indian rice dish). *Khichri* is the word normally used to describe a dish of rice and daal cooked together.

> *55g (2oz) toor daal (deep yellow lentils)*
> *225g (8oz) basmati rice*
> *3 tablespoons oil*
> *4 each of cardamom pods, cinnamon sticks, bay leaves and cloves*
> *(whole garam masala)*

¼ teaspoon turmeric

salt

Soak the daal for 2 hours. In a large bowl, soak the rice for 30 minutes, then rinse it until the water runs clear and loses its chalkiness. In a pan (one that will fit into your oven) with a tightly fitting lid, heat the oil to very hot. In order to ensure the oil is hot enough, drop in a clove or cardamom pod from the whole *garam masala*. If it sizzles and splutters at once, add the remaining spices from the whole *garam masala*. If it turns very dark, reduce the heat and add the remaining spices after 1 minute. Now add the rice, daal and 568ml (1 pint) of water. Add the turmeric and salt and bring to the boil. Immediately reduce the heat to very low and cover with the tightly fitting lid. Cook for 20 minutes, without uncovering. Meanwhile, preheat the oven to 200°C, 400°F, gas mark 6. After 20 minutes, transfer the pan, without uncovering it, to the oven for a further 20 minutes. Serve immediately.

CHICKEN TIKKA BIRYANI
Delicately flavoured rice with marinated chicken pieces

This is a recipe I have developed for those of my pupils who have eaten this dish in Indian restaurants in the UK and want to know how to make it themselves. This is not an authentic Indian recipe but it has proved, nonetheless, to be a great success. Serve with cachumbar (raw vegetable relish) or raita.

> *450g (1lb) chicken tikkas (see page 40)*
> *450g (1lb) basmati rice*
> *6 tablespoons oil*
> *2 medium onions, peeled and finely chopped*
> *1 tablespoon tomato purée*
> *½ teaspoon chilli powder*
> *3 each of cardamom pods, cinnamon sticks, bay leaves and cloves*
> *(whole garam masala)*
> *2 tablespoons natural yogurt*
> *pinch saffron threads soaked in 1 tablespoon water*
> *pinch powdered orange food colouring dissolved in 1 teaspoon warm water*
> *or 1 teaspoon liquid orange food colouring*
> *¼ teaspoon garam masala powder (see Stockists)*
> *salt*

First, prepare the chicken *tikkas* according to the recipe on page 40. In a large bowl, soak the rice for 30 minutes, then rinse it until the water runs clear and loses its chalkiness. Preheat the oven to 200°C, 400°F, gas mark 6. Meanwhile, in a pan with a tightly fitting lid, heat 5 tablespoons of the oil and fry the onions until golden brown.

Add the tomato purée, chilli powder, salt and 2 of each of the elements of the whole *garam masala*. Fry the mixture, adding a small amount of the yogurt at a time, waiting for one lot to be completely absorbed before adding the next, stirring briskly to prevent curdling. Add the chicken *tikkas* and simmer over a low heat for 15-20 minutes.

This is not meant to have a sauce, but neither must it be too dry; some moisture is needed for the next stage (the *dum* stage), so add a little water if it gets too dry. Then transfer to an ovenproof dish with a tightly fitting lid and set aside.

Now fill a pan with plenty of water and bring to the boil. Add salt, the remaining whole *garam masala* and the rice, and cook until the rice is parboiled (about 5 minutes – the grains should be partly cooked).

Drain the rice, arrange it on top of the chicken and speckle with the remaining oil, the saffron-infused water and the food colouring. Seal the dish tightly and place in the oven for 20 minutes. Then reduce the heat to 150°C, 300°F, gas mark 2 and leave for a further 30 minutes. Garnish with the *garam masala* powder and serve immediately.

LAMB PATHANI BIRYANI
Delicately flavoured rice with lamb, spinach, fenugreek and sweet corn

A green biryani with deliciously subtle flavours, this is best served with raita. The Pathan are a warrior tribe from northern Pakistan; I don't know for certain, but this could be a dish from that area, hence its name.

450g (1lb) basmati rice
6 tablespoons oil
2 onions, peeled and finely chopped
3 each of cardamom pods, cinnamon sticks, bay leaves and cloves (whole garam masala)
450g (1lb) leg lamb, cut into cubes
6 teaspoons hara masala (chilli and coriander paste; see page 31)
2 teaspoons puréed ginger
2 teaspoons puréed garlic/10 cloves garlic, peeled and crushed
1 teaspoon cumin powder
¼ teaspoon turmeric
125g (4½oz) spinach (frozen or fresh), chopped
125g (4½oz) fenugreek (frozen or fresh), chopped
125g (4½oz) sweet corn, cooked
salt

In a large bowl, soak the rice for 30 minutes, then rinse it until the water runs clear and loses its chalkiness. Preheat the oven to 200°C, 400°F, gas mark 6. In large pan, heat the oil and fry the onions until translucent. Add 2 of each of the elements of the whole *garam masala*. Add the lamb and fry for 2 minutes. Add the *hara masala*, ginger, garlic, cumin powder, turmeric and salt. Fry over a high heat until you can see the oil begin to separate from the spices at the edges of the pan, adding a little water from time to time to prolong the frying and stop the spices from sticking and burning. Then add 1 litre (1¾pints) of water, and leave to simmer until the lamb is tender (about 50 minutes). (Check from time to time to make sure it isn't drying out – top up with water if it is.) Next, add the spinach and fenugreek and leave to simmer until the mixture is fairly dry and the fenugreek and spinach are well combined with the spices. Then transfer to an ovenproof dish with a tightly fitting lid and set aside. Now fill a pan with plenty of water and bring to the boil. Add salt, the remaining whole *garam masala* and the rice, and cook until the rice is parboiled (about 5 minutes – the grains should be partly cooked). Drain the rice, arrange it on top of the lamb mixture, cover with the lid and place in the oven or 30 minutes. Then reduce the heat to 150°C, 300°F, gas mark 2 and leave for a further 30 minutes. Serve garnished with the sweet corn.

❧ BREAD

Bread or rice are the accompaniments served with most Indian meals, and most traditional Indian breads are unleavened (flat). To enjoy them at their best, eat them immediately after they have been baked, while they are still wonderfully fresh and piping hot.

Indian bread is generally made from ground wholemeal (*atta*), though sorghum (*jowar*) and millet (*bajra*) are also used. Chapatis and *parathas* (though not *aloo parathas*) can be half-baked, then stored in the freezer for up to 1 month. When you want to serve them, simply defrost and fully bake. Thicker chapatis freeze better than thinner ones.

CHAPATIS

Generally, chapatis are cooked on a *tawa*, which is a slightly concave thick griddle pan made of cast iron. Use a flat heavy-bottomed frying pan if you do not have a *tawa*, though it may be wise to invest in one (to find out where to get hold of one, see Stockists), as they are versatile and can be used to make other Indian dishes, in particular *tawa gosht* (literally, meat cooked in a *tawa*).

> *700g (1lb 9oz) atta (chapati flour, see Stockists; or same amount wholemeal and plain flour combined in equal quantity), plus extra to dust*
>
> *4 tablespoons oil*

Sieve the *atta* into a large clean dry bowl, make a well in the centre and pour in 200ml (7fl oz) of water. Knead well for 3 minutes, until fairly soft. Set aside, covered with a moist cloth, for 30 minutes. After this time, divide the dough into 12 portions and roll into balls. Flatten each one, and on a lightly floured surface, roll them out to form thin round pancakes about 18cm (7in) in diameter. Heat a *tawa* or flat heavy-bottomed frying pan until it is very hot and place 1 chapati in the middle. Cook on one side for 2-3 minutes, then turn over. Move it round with a piece of rolled-up cloth, pressing it gently all over (this helps it to cook evenly). When it is speckled with brown spots, remove and coat with half a teaspoon of oil on each side. Set aside and wrap in kitchen foil while you cook the remaining chapatis.

PURIS

These deliciously soft, deep-fried discs are particularly suited to accompanying vegetables, especially potatoes.

> *700g (1 lb 9oz) atta (chapati flour, see Stockists; or same amount wholemeal and plain flour combined in equal quantity), plus extra to dust*
>
> *oil, for deep-frying*
>
> *salt*

Sieve the *atta* and salt together into a large clean dry bowl, make a well in the centre and slowly pour in 200ml (7fl oz) of warm water. Knead well for 3 minutes, until fairly soft.

Set aside, covered with a moist cloth, for 30 minutes. After this time, divide the dough into about 18 small portions, and on a lightly floured surface roll them out into discs about 10cm (4in) in diameter. Next, heat enough oil in a *karai* or wok-like pan to deep-fry the *puris*. Deep-fry them until golden brown, turning them over once (this will make them puff up). Drain on kitchen paper before serving.

PARATHAS

A variation on chapatis, these are best served immediately after cooking. However, if made in advance they can be wrapped in kitchen foil, then reheated on a *tawa* or flat heavy-bottomed frying pan, or in a microwave.

> *350g (12oz) plain flour, plus extra to dust*
>
> *350g (12oz) atta (chapati flour, see Stockists; or same amount wholemeal and plain flour combined in equal quantity)*
>
> *125ml (4fl oz) oil*
>
> *salt*

Sieve the plain flour, *atta* and salt together into a large clean dry bowl, make a well in the centre and pour in 200ml (7fl oz) of water. Knead well for 3 minutes, until fairly soft. Set aside, covered with a moist cloth, for 30 minutes. After this time, divide the dough into 8 portions and, on a lightly floured surface, roll them out into discs about 10cm (4in) in diameter. Coat one side of each with a small amount of oil, fold over and roll each one into a ball. Once more on a floured surface, again roll them out into discs, this time measuring approximately 20cm (8in) in diameter. Heat a *tawa* or flat heavy-bottomed frying pan and place one *paratha* in the centre, turning it over after 1 minute. Then drizzle one tablespoon of oil around the edges and shallow-fry until the *paratha* is golden brown. Remove and set aside, wrapped in kitchen foil, while you cook the remaining *parathas*.

ALOO PARATHAS
Parathas stuffed with potatoes

> *To make the parathas*
>
> *350g (12oz) plain flour, plus extra to dust*
>
> *350g (12oz) atta (chapati flour, see Stockists; or same amount wholemeal and plain flour combined in equal quantity)*
>
> *125ml (4fl oz) oil*
>
> *salt*

To make the potato filling

4 medium potatoes, weighing about 750g (1lb 10oz)

1 green chilli, deseeded and finely chopped

1 tablespoon puréed ginger

15g (½oz) finely chopped fresh coriander leaves

¼ teaspoon chilli powder

¼ teaspoon cumin powder

salt

First cook the potatoes in their skins in a pan of boiling salted water until tender. Meanwhile, sieve the plain flour, *atta* and salt together into a large clean dry bowl, make a well in the centre and pour in 200ml (7fl oz) of water. Knead well for 3 minutes, until fairly soft. Set aside, covered with a moist cloth, for 30 minutes.

When the potatoes are ready, drain, cool, peel and mash them. Add all the other ingredients for the filling to the potatoes, combine and divide into 8 portions. Now divide the *paratha* dough into 8 portions and, on a lightly floured surface, roll them out into discs about 12cm (4½in) in diameter. Coat one side of each with a small amount of oil.

Place a portion of the potato filling in the middle and cover with the surrounding dough. Flatten again and, once more on a lightly floured surface, again roll them out into discs, this time measuring approximately 20cm (8in) in diameter. Heat a *tawa* or flat heavy-bottomed frying pan and place one *paratha* in the centre, turning it over after 1 minute. Then drizzle one tablespoon of oil around the edges and shallow-fry until the *paratha* is speckled brown. Remove and set aside, wrapped in kitchen foil, while you cook the remaining *parathas*. Serve with raita.

NAAN

Ideally, these popular breads should be baked in a *tandoor* (traditional clay oven).

450g (1lb) plain flour

¼ teaspoon bicarbonate of soda

1 teaspoon baking powder

2½ teaspoons sugar

2 tablespoons natural yogurt

3 tablespoons milk

1 egg

5 teaspoons oil

atta (chapati flour, see Stockists), to dust

1 teaspoon nigella seeds (kalonji)

1 tablespoon butter, melted, plus extra for greasing
salt

Sieve the flour, 1 teaspoon of salt, the bicarbonate of soda and baking powder into a bowl and make a well in the centre. In a separate bowl, whisk together the sugar, yogurt, milk and egg. Gradually pour 125ml (4fl oz) of water into the well in the flour mixture and mix in. Knead to make a dough. Then slowly add the egg mixture and knead the dough for a further 7 minutes. It should be soft and not stick to your fingers. Moisten you hands with water if it is very sticky. Now place in a bowl, cover with a moist cloth and set aside for 15 minutes. After this time, knead the oil into the dough, cover once more with a moist cloth and set aside for 2 hours for it to rise. Preheat the oven to 190°C, 375°F, gas mark 5. Divide the dough into 6 portions and roll into balls. Gently flatten them with your hands on a surface lightly dusted with *atta* and sprinkle each one with a few nigella seeds. Flatten them further to form discs measuring about 13cm (5in) in diameter, then gently pull each one to make an oval shape. Place them on a greased baking tray and bake in the oven for 10 minutes. If you have a *tandoor*, they should be baked for 3-4 minutes on the side of the oven. As soon as they are ready, baste each naan with the melted butter and serve immediately.

ACCOMPANIMENTS

In addition to rice and bread, there is one element of an Indian meal without which it would not be complete – the accompaniments. These are a selection of relishes and side dishes that serve to complement the flavours of the main meal (chutneys), refresh the palate (cachumbars – raw vegetable relishes) and lessen the heat of the spices (raitas). Easy to make, they will add a touch of authenticity to any Indian menu.

CHUTNEYS

An assortment of chutneys and *achaars* (pickles) will be found accompanying most Indian meals. These enhance the flavours of the food, and in some cases they provide spice and heat to what might be otherwise bland dishes. Some of the hotter chutneys are not for the faint-hearted, and I would suggest a cautious approach with these! Chutneys originate from the word *chaat-na*, which literally means 'to lick'.

PUDINA CHUTNEY
Mint chutney

Sometimes this is referred to as *hara chutney*. *Hara* means 'green' in Hindi.

> *25g (1oz) fresh coriander leaves*
> *60g (2¼oz) fresh mint leaves*
> *1 green chilli, deseeded*
> *2 cloves garlic, peeled*
> *1 small onion, peeled and roughly chopped*
> *1 teaspoon sugar*
> *3 tablespoons lemon juice*
> *salt*

Put 4 tablespoons of water and all the ingredients, except the lemon juice, into a food processor and whiz to form a paste. Add the lemon juice. Store in the fridge for up to 2 days. Bring back to room temperature before serving.

QUICK MINT SAUCE

> *1 tablespoon ready-made mint sauce*
> *250g (9oz) natural yogurt*

Mix the ingredients together to create a refreshing dip for poppadoms (thin fried or roasted bread) and *bhajiyas* (deep-fried vegetable fritters). Store in the fridge for up to 2 days.

MITHA CHUTNEY
Date and tamarind chutney

Sweet and sour, with a delicious tangy flavour, this can be added to *dahi vadas* (lentil donuts with yogurt) and *papri chaat* (crisp flour discs topped with potatoes) and is also used as a dip for *bhajiyas* (deep-fried vegetable fritters). Store in the fridge for up to five days.

> *9oz (250g) pitted dates*
> *2 tablespoons concentrated tamarind paste (see Stockists)*
> *¼ teaspoon chilli powder*
> *¼ teaspoon cumin powder*
> *15g (½oz) finely chopped fresh coriander leaves*

Heat 850ml (1½ pints) of water, add the dates and bring to the boil, letting them simmer for 5 minutes. Add the tamarind paste, chilli powder and cumin powder and cook for another 5 minutes. The mixture should be quite thick but still a bit runny (viscous, like honey). Remove from the heat and pour through a sieve, working the mixture so as to get as much of it through as possible. The thickness of the paste will depend on personal preference; if you like it runny, simply add more water. Garnish with the fresh coriander just before serving.

NARIYAL KA CHUTNEY
Coconut and coriander chutney

A fresh, coarsely textured chutney, this goes well with kebabs and *bhajiyas* (deep-fried vegetable fritters) and can be stored in the fridge for up to two days.

> *55g (2oz) desiccated coconut*
> *25g (1oz) chopped fresh coriander leaves*
> *1 green chilli, deseeded*
> *2 cloves garlic, peeled*
> *1 teaspoon sugar*
> *3 tablespoons lemon juice*
> *salt*

Put 100ml (3½fl oz) of water together with all the ingredients, except the lemon juice, in a processor and whiz to form a smooth paste. Mix in the lemon juice and serve.

CACHUMBARS

Made with a variety of raw, fresh vegetables, these relishes are like a cross between a salsa and a small side salad, and are normally seasoned with lemon juice and salt. They are particularly refreshing when eaten with spicy dishes. Green chillies or red chilli powder can be added if a spicy *cachumbar* is preferred, but don't need to be added if the main dish itself is spicy. *Cachumbars* are usually served with biryanis (delicately flavoured rice with marinated meat) and pilaus.

ONION AND TOMATO CACHUMBAR

> *2 tomatoes*
> *2 small onions or 4 shallots, peeled*
> *1 green chilli, deseeded*
> *15g (½oz) fresh coriander leaves*
> *2 tablespoons lemon juice or vinegar*
> *salt*

Chop the tomatoes, onions or shallots, green chilli and coriander leaves very finely. Add the salt and lemon juice or vinegar and serve immediately.

CUCUMBER AND ONION CACHUMBAR

> *½ small cucumber, halved lengthways*
> *1 medium onion, peeled and halved lengthways (from root to tip)*
> *1 green chilli, deseeded*
> *15g (½oz) finely chopped fresh coriander leaves*
> *2 tablespoons lemon juice*
> *salt*

Finely slice the cucumber and onion (the pieces should be thin and semi circular). Chop the green chilli and combine with the cucumber and onion slices, together with the fresh coriander, salt and lemon juice. Serve immediately.

RAITAS

The basis of all raitas is yogurt, and these cooling accompaniments provide a healthy addition to any meal, as well as tone down the heat of the spiciest dishes. They can be made with a variety of vegetables, and are normally seasoned with salt and chilli powder; sometimes sugar is added if the yogurt is very sour. You can be quite innovative in the ingredients you add to the base: aubergine (eggplant) slices, crisply fried or even smoked and puréed, work very well, as does puréed avocado. Usually garnished with a sprinkling of cumin powder and fresh coriander, raitas are served with biryanis (delicately flavoured rice with marinated meat) and pilaus.

KHEERA KA RAITA
Cucumber raita

> *500g (1lb 2oz) natural yogurt*
> *½ teaspoon sugar*
> *½ large cucumber, grated*
> *15g (½oz) finely chopped fresh coriander leaves*
> *pinch chilli powder*
> *pinch cumin powder*
> *salt*

Briefly whisk the yogurt to loosen it and add salt and the sugar. Add the grated cucumber and combine. Garnish with the fresh coriander, chilli powder and cumin powder and serve immediately.

ALOO KA RAITA
Potato raita

> *2 medium potatoes, weighing about 375g (13oz)*
> *500g (1lb 2oz] natural yogurt*
> *15g (½oz) finely chopped fresh coriander leaves*
> *pinch chilli powder*
> *pinch cumin powder*
> *salt*

First cook the potatoes in their skins in a pan of boiling salted water until tender. Drain, cool, peel and dice. Set aside. Whisk the yogurt to loosen it and add salt and the potatoes. Garnish with the fresh coriander, chilli powder and cumin powder.

Desserts

Rich, creamy creations, delicious and decadent, from kulfi, an Indian dessert known to many, to the less widely known but equally irresistible shahi tukra and firni. The meal may be coming to an end, but one very special element remains.

SHAHI TUKRA
Rich, creamy bread pudding with saffron and cardamom

Known as 'the dessert of the kings' (*shahi* means 'royal' and *tukra* means 'a piece'), this is a dish of Mogul origin and is particularly popular among the Muslim communities of India. It is not unlike bread-and-butter pudding and has a distinctive flavour, which comes from frying the bread before cooking it in milk. It is garnished lavishly with nuts and, if available, sheets of silver leaf (*varq*).

When I was a little girl, *shahi tukra* would always be homemade, and was served only on special occasions in individual portions. As children, my siblings and I always used to hope there would be several of these left over after a dinner party, so we could enjoy them chilled the next day.

4 slices white bread, crusts left on
200ml (7fl oz) oil
568ml (1 pint) milk
3 tablespoons white sugar
¼ teaspoon cardamom powder
150ml (5fl oz) double cream
pinch saffron threads
silver leaf (varq; see Stockists), to garnish (optional)
pistachio nuts, finely chopped, to garnish

Fry the bread in the oil until pale brown. Remove and set aside. Then heat the milk in a frying pan large enough to fit all 4 pieces of bread in one layer and add the sugar and cardamom powder. Place the slices of bread in the frying pan, laying them in a single layer, and cook over a very low heat until the bread has soaked up all the milk.

Now add the double cream and saffron and leave to cook for a few more minutes. The bread should have soaked up most of the liquid but a little creamy sauce should remain. Place each slice of bread with some of the creamy sauce on a small dessert plate and leave to cool down. This will take about 30 minutes.

When you are ready to serve the *shahi tukra*, apply some silver leaf to each portion (if using) and garnish with the nuts. Serve chilled or at room temperature.

PINEAPPLE HALWA
Pineapple, cream and saffron pudding

85g (3oz) butter
850g (1lb 14oz) tinned pineapple slices
450g (1lb) tinned crushed pineapple

pinch saffron threads

¼ teaspoon cardamom powder

400g (14oz) tinned evaporated milk

300ml (10fl oz) double cream

25g (1oz) pistachio nuts, chopped, to garnish

Heat the butter in a pan, add the pineapple slices and the juice from the tin and fry for 3 minutes. Add the crushed pineapple, saffron, cardamom powder and the evaporated milk and bring to the boil.

Reduce the heat and let the mixture cook for 30 minutes, until all the liquid has been absorbed. It may curdle, which is fine; the only difference will be in the texture, but it will still taste as it should.

When all the liquid has been absorbed, remove from heat and leave to cool. When it is still warm, stir in the double cream and garnish with pistachio nuts. Serve at once.

CARROT HALWA
Carrot, cream and saffron pudding

Very popular in India, this is normally made using milk from which all the water has been evaporated, leaving a thick creamy mixture known as *mawa* or *khoya*. Since such high-quality cream is available in the West, I have used it here to speed up the process.

1lb (450g) carrots, finely grated

1 litre (1¾ pints) milk

6 cardamom pods, left whole

5 tablespoons caster sugar

pinch saffron threads

125g (4½oz) butter

300ml (10fl oz) double cream

silver leaf (varq; see Stockists), to garnish (optional)

25g (1oz) pistachio nuts, chopped, to garnish

In a pan, place the grated carrots, milk, cardamom pods, caster sugar and saffron and bring to the boil. Reduce the heat and cook until there is no liquid left. Then, in a separate pan, heat the butter and fry the carrot mixture in it until it turns reddish brown in colour.

Add the cream and leave to cook for 5 minutes over a low heat. Then remove from the heat, fish out the cardamom pods, apply the silver leaf on top (if using), garnish with the pistachio nuts and serve.

SEERKHURMA
Rich milk drink

Traditionally, this drink is served in Muslim homes on the occasion of Eid (a religious festival), and the recipe varies from one family to the next. Some prefer it to be so thick it has to be eaten with a spoon; others make it more like a milkshake.

Our family cook in India would arrive before dawn to begin preparations for his version, as it had to be ready for Eid breakfast, and throughout the day people who visited us would have a choice of *seerkhurma* or Coca-Cola. Needless to say, most opted for the former! The following is an adaptation of our cook's recipe. His did not include cream or evaporated milk; instead he used milk that he had reduced by slowly cooking it. He also incorporated several dried fruits that are, unfortunately, difficult to obtain outside India. One cup of this is never enough, but two is one too many! It is yummy, but very heavy.

85g (3oz) butter
225g (8oz) vermicelli
125g (4½oz) raisins
568ml (1 pint) whole milk
400g (14oz) tinned evaporated milk
300ml (10fl oz) single cream
about 4 tablespoons sugar (adjust to taste)
pinch saffron threads
6 tablespoons chopped pistachio nuts

In a frying pan, heat the butter and fry the vermicelli and raisins for a couple of minutes, until they turn a darker colour. Set aside. In a large pan, combine the milk, evaporated milk, cream and sugar and cook for 15 minutes over a low heat. Now add the saffron, raisins and vermicelli and continue to cook for a further 15 minutes. Finally, add the pistachio nuts. Serve hot or chilled.

KULFI
Indian ice cream

Indian ice cream is perhaps the best way to define kulfi. Originally, it was made with milk that was slowly evaporated and reduced to a creamy consistency, and at first only saffron and nuts were added. Today, however, all kinds of ingredients are added to make different varieties of kulfi. When I was growing up in India, the *kulfiwalla* (kulfi man) was, as his name suggests, the manufacturer and purveyor of these treats. He stored them in sealed aluminium cones and carried them around in a container full of ice. Kulfi is now mass produced, and I feel today's versions cannot compare to the ones made by the *kulfiwalla*. The following is a very quick and easy recipe, which takes advantage of the fact that so many different types of milk are now easily available. Kulfi moulds can be purchased from Indian food shops (see Stockists).

300ml (10fl oz) double cream
400g (14oz) tinned evaporated milk
200g (7oz) tinned sweetened condensed milk
¼ teaspoon vanilla essence

Optional extras:
For malai kulfi
pinch cardamom powder and pinch saffron threads dissolved in 1 tablespoon hot milk

For pistachio kulfi
125g (4½oz) pistachio nuts, chopped, and a drop of liquid green food colouring

For rich chocolate kulfi
3 tablespoons cocoa powder dissolved in 2 tablespoons hot milk

For mango kulfi
200g (7oz) tinned mango pulp (preferably from Alphonso mangoes)

Whisk the double cream until it thickens slightly. Add the evaporated milk, condensed milk and vanilla essence and continue to whisk for 2 minutes. At this point, add any of the optional extras your require. The mixture should be thick and creamy. Pour into kulfi moulds and seal or pour into an old ice-cream carton or freezer box and leave to set in the freezer for a couple of hours. Remove the mixture from the freezer, stir (to prevent ice forming), then return to the freezer for a couple more hours. Repeat once or twice more. Transfer to the fridge for 30-45 minutes before serving, in order for it to soften up.

MANGO MOUSSE

A lighter change from traditional heavy Indian desserts, this is easy to whip up and refreshes the palate.

300ml (10fl oz) double cream
850g (1lb 14oz) tinned mango pulp (preferably from Alphonso mangoes)
or same quantity puréed mango (preferably Alphonso mangoes)
few almond flakes, to garnish

Whip the cream until thick. Add the mango pulp or puréed mango and whip together, to combine. Spoon into ice-cream cups and chill. Decorate with the almond flakes just before serving.

KHEER
Indian rice pudding

Definitely not to be made if you are on a diet! This is the traditional Indian recipe for rice pudding, flavoured with saffron and cardamom.

225g (8oz) rice
568ml (1 pint) milk
175g (6oz) sugar
1 teaspoon cardamom powder
2 teaspoons saffron threads
400g (14oz) tinned evaporated milk
300ml (10fl oz) double cream
4 tablespoons chopped pistachio nuts, to garnish

In a large bowl, soak the rice for 30 minutes, then rinse it until the water runs clear and loses its chalkiness. Then place it in a pan with 1 litre (1¾ pints) of cold water, bring to the boil and boil for about 30 minutes, until well cooked, then whisk it for 1 minute to achieve a porridge-like consistency. Boil the milk to reduce it by half. Then add the rice together with the sugar, cardamom powder, saffron and evaporated milk. Leave it to cook over a very low heat for 15 minutes, stirring to prevent it sticking to the bottom of the pan. Now stir in the cream and leave to cook for another 5 minutes. It should be a rich, creamy colour. Pour into a serving bowl, leave to cool and garnish with the nuts. Serve warm or cold.

FIRNI
Rice pudding with a difference!

A delicious variation of *kheer*, this is bowl-scrapingly good! It is usually set and served in earthenware bowls, which seem to lend it a special flavour and help to absorb the moisture, making the dish nice and dry. It can be decorated with silver leaf (*varq*). In India, this is one dessert we normally sent for from restaurants because of the unique taste imparted by the earthenware bowls. It is particularly good chilled. If you cannot obtain earthenware bowls, set it in individual shallow bowls.

115g (4oz) rice

700ml (1¼ pints) whole milk

115g (4oz) sugar

pinch saffron threads

5 cardamom pods or ¼ teaspoon cardamom powder

125ml (4fl oz) double cream

2 drops rose-water

silver leaf (varq; see Stockists), to garnish (optional)

2 tablespoons finely chopped pistachio nuts, to garnish

In a large bowl, soak the rice in 1.5 litres (2¾ pints) of water for 30 minutes. Drain the rice, then make a paste of it by putting it in a blender with a few tablespoons of water. Heat the milk, add the rice and sugar and leave to cook over a low heat for about 25 minutes. Add the saffron and continue to cook, whisking if necessary to ensure there are no lumps.

Next, if using the cardamom pods, remove the seeds from the husks by hand and add to the rice-and-milk mixture, or simply stir in the cardamom powder. Now add the cream and cook over a low heat until the mixture is thick and looks like custard (5-10 minutes).

Remove from the heat, add the rose-water, pour into individual shallow or earthenware bowls and leave to cool down and set (about 45 minutes). When they are set, apply silver leaf (*varq*) to the top of each one (if using), garnish with the pistachio nuts and serve.

LASSI
Refreshing sweet or savoury yogurt drink

> ***For sweet lassi***
> *200g (7oz) natural yogurt*
> *4 teaspoons sugar*

> ***For savoury lassi***
> *200g (7oz) natural yogurt*
> *pinch freshly ground black pepper*
> *pinch cumin powder*
> *salt*

To make either lassi, combine all the ingredients with 400ml (14fl oz) of water and serve with ice.

APPENDICES

APPENDIX 1
Menu suggestions

Menu 1

Gosht-e-Mehboob

Dill pilau

Gujarati-style potatoes

Tarka daal

Kheera ka raita

Mango mousse

Menu 2

Chicken tikka masala

Jeera pilau

Aab gosht

Quick green beans

Aloo ka raita

Firni

Menu 3

Seekh kebabs

Daal gosht

Brown rice

Quick spicy sweet corn

Cachumbar

Kheer

Menu 4

Smoked salmon tikkas

Zafrani murg

Vegetable pilau

Onion bhajiyas

Cachumbar

Kulfi

Summer lunch

Dahi vadas

Quick mixed vegetables

Aloo ka raita

Tawa gosht

Dill pilau

Naan

Kulfi or mango mousse

Brunch

Papri chaat

Anda ka kheema

Chicken malai kebabs

Aloo, mattar aur tamatar

Puris

Pineapple halwa

Royal banquet

Bagara baigan

Zafrani murg

Lamb pathani biryani

Parathas

Kheera ka raita

Shahi tukra

Kids' menu

Cutlets (meat or vegetable)

Anda ka kheema

Kuku paka

Murgi ka salna

Gujarati-style potatoes

Puris

Vegetable pilau

Canapé menu

Papri chaat

Assorted bhajiyas

Aloo tikkis

Shami kebabs

Pudina chutney

VEGETARIAN

Menu 1

Aloo vadas

Vegetable pilau

Chana batata

Stuffed green peppers

Cachumbar

Kheer

Menu 2

Mattar paneer

Tarka daal

Jeera pilau

Bhindi ki bhaji

Parathas or chapatis

Kheera ka raita

Carrot halwa

Menu 3

Dahi ki curry

Bhuni khichri

Sag aloo

Bagara baigan

Chapatis

Cachumbar

Firni

APPENDIX 2
If there is food, can drink be far behind?

What does one drink with Indian food? Drinking alcohol with food is not part of the Indian tradition and in most homes tepid water is drunk, during and after the meal. Soft drinks were seen as an unnecessary extravagance when I was growing up.

At parties it is customary to serve beer, gin and whisky, though wine drinking is only now making an appearance with the establishment of a few wineries. It is a commonly held belief in the West that only beer or lager are compatible with a curry, yet there are several wines that really lend themselves to Indian food.

The difficulty lies in the fact that most Indian meals consist of several different dishes, some mild and some rather hot, and it is deciding how hot the meal is going to be that will dictate the choice of wine. Chardonnay goes well with the milder creamy dishes, while something at the hotter end of the scale will need a Portuguese red or an Australian Shiraz.

In India, lassis are very popular summer drinks. Normally seasoned with freshly ground black pepper, cumin powder and fresh mint leaves, they are both cooling and refreshing. Mango lassi, which is popular in the West, is rarely served in India, as mangoes are only available for a short period and it is considered a waste to dilute the food known in India as the king of fruits with yogurt!

APPENDIX 3
'Your food shall be your medicine'
Hippocrates

The food we eat and the spices we use play a vital role in the maintenance of good health. One leading nutritionist has even gone as far as to say that the right kind of food is the single most important factor in the enjoyment of good health, while the wrong kind of food is the single most important factor in the promotion of disease. Although extensive details of foods and their benefits is outside the orbit of this book, here I have listed commonly used Indian herbs and spices and their medicinal attributes. I have made a particular effort to include all those with aphrodisiac qualities, in response to the many requests made by men attending my cookery seminars!

Aniseed: Said to aid digestion.

Asafoetida: Known as the food of the Gods by the Persians. Though used in England in the 18th century, it is now rarely used in Western cuisine, but adds a wonderful garlicky flavour to many Indian dishes. Is said to counteract flatulence.

Bay leaf: Mixed with cinnamon and cardamom, is said to relieve respiratory congestion.

Black pepper: Said to burn toxins in the body and, together with ginger and chilli peppers, can relieve respiratory congestion.

Caraway seeds: Said to relieve colic and improve digestion.

Cardamom pods: Identified as having aphrodisiac qualities in that classic of Oriental literature, *Tales from the Thousand and One Nights*. Said to freshen breath and combat nausea, headaches, fevers, coughs, asthma, piles and eye diseases.

Chillies: Astonishingly, eating hot chillies in a hot climate can help keep the body cool, as they encourage sweating. Said to be good for digestive ailments.

Cinnamon: Cinnamon oil has been used to treat toothache and headaches, as well as impotence.

Cloves: Used since ancient times for medicinal purposes and employed to treat, among other things, toothache, fevers, dyspepsia and spleen, kidney, stomach and intestinal disorders. Has also been used in toothpaste and as an antiseptic.

Coriander (seeds and leaves): The seeds have been prescribed for constipation, insomnia and pregnant women. Coriander leaves are said to remove heat from the system, especially from the areas of the eyes and intestines.

Dill (fresh): Used by the Egyptians, Greeks and Romans for medicinal purposes. According to the Ayurveda, helps to relieve gas, colic and hiccups and to control diarrhoea. Said to increase and medicate breast-milk to help strengthen a baby's digestion.

Fennel (seeds): Said to be good for digestion, to sweeten breath and, when boiled in water, to calm inflamed and tired eyes. Also said to prevent gallstones. Fennel oil is a decongestant and used to treat coughs.

Fenugreek: Recommended in the 11th century by the Arab physician Avicenna to treat diabetes. Also said to be good for lowering blood pressure, and used in the oral contraceptive pill and in veterinary medicine. Also said to improve the digestive, respiratory and nervous systems, purify the skin and tone the whole system. Fenugreek-seed paste is said to purify boils and abscesses and to prevent premature hair loss when used as a shampoo.

Garlic: Cultivated since prehistoric times and said to have been used by the builders of the pyramids in Egypt to keep up their strength. Reputed to cure many ailments, including nosebleeds, skin problems, coughs, colds, bronchitis and asthma. Said to dilate blood vessels and reduce high blood pressure. Often prescribed to prevent coronary heart disease. The list is endless and legendary. A libido booster, too, apparently!

Ginger: Excellent for counteracting flatulence, hence its use with lentils (daals) and cauliflower. Ginger is the supreme toxin digestant in the *Ayurveda* (Sanskrit writings in the ancient Hindu art of healing) and, made into a strong tea with castor oil, is said to treat rheumatism and rheumatoid arthritis. The Ayurvedics used it to preserve food, as a digestive aid and as a spiritual and physical cleanser. Is viewed as an aphrodisiac in traditional Chinese medicine. Reputed to help with anaemia and liver complaints.

Onions: A trusted traditional home remedy. Said to protect teeth and to cure alopecia, asthma, laryngitis, heatstroke and rheumatism, among other ailments.

Also regarded as an aphrodisiac and a symbol of fertility.

Peppercorns: The king of spices. Said to be particularly good for digestive ailments.

Poppy seeds: Said to have been used in ancient times by Olympic athletes to provide an instant burst of energy.

Saffron: Widely regarded as an aphrodisiac, especially when dissolved in milk; also said to relieve respiratory congestion. Is used in pastes to improve the complexion and is reputed to purify the mind.

Sesame seeds: Claimed by early writers to be an antidote to lizard bites; the Roman historian Pliny maintained they prevented vomiting. Used in Africa today to treat dysentery and a number of stomach ailments.

Tamarind: Meaning 'date of India'. Boiled in water and sweetened is said to cool fever. Combined with other ingredients is said to relieve the effects of alcohol. Used to increase appetite and digestion. Has a laxative effect.

Turmeric: Has well-known antiseptic qualities. Said to slow bleeding when applied to wounds. Used extensively to improve the complexion and as a depilatory; also said to cure itching, skin diseases and conjunctivitis; fumes from smoked turmeric are said to treat fainting, hiccups and asthma.

APPENDIX 4
The Indian spice kitchen and the essential spice kitchen

Asafoetida (*heeng*):
Dried gum resin from the hardened sap of the giant fennel plant. A powerful seasoning, used in minute quantities. Has a slightly ammoniac smell, which disappears on cooking, imparting a garlicky flavour to food. Often used in vegetarian food; is reputed to help digestion.

Bay leaf (*tej patta*):
Strongly aromatic; can be used fresh or dried. When added to hot oil, releases its full flavour. Adds a wonderful aroma to rice and meat preparations.

Cardamom (*elaichi*):
An ancient ingredient said to have grown in the Hanging Gardens of Babylon. Features prominently in dishes of Mogul origin; adds aroma and fragrance to biryanis (delicately flavoured rice with marinated meat) and sweet dishes. Available in pods (green or black), as loose seeds or powder. My own preference is for the green pods. One of the ingredients in *garam masala* (a spice mixture used in many Indian dishes).

Cinnamon (*dalchini*):
Another ancient ingredient. Once a rare and expensive spice; said to have been used by Moses to anoint the Ark of the Covenant. Today it is easily available and affordable and used for its flavour and the aroma it imparts to meat and rice dishes. Available in sticks or powdered form; the stick used whole imparts more flavour and can be discarded once the dish is ready (it is not meant to be eaten).

Clarified butter (ghee):
Traditionally Indians prefer to use this instead of oil, as it gives more flavour to food. Recent health concerns with regard to cholesterol have prompted some people to change to using oil instead of ghee. However, it has some unique properties: it has a cooling effect on the body and brings out the best in the ingredients it is cooked with.

Clove (*lavang*): The dried unopened buds of the clove tree. Used in cooking, medicine and for making perfume.

Coriander leaves (*dhania patta*): My favourite herb. Fresh green coriander leaves are a welcome addition to every Indian dish. They should always be very finely chopped when used to garnish dishes, to release the full flavour. Ground with mint and chillies, they make a wonderful marinade or basis for a sauce. I believe you can never add too much coriander to any Indian preparation. In fact, any amount can be added without fear of ruining the dish, something that can't be said about any other herb!

Coriander seeds (*sabut dhania*): Small round seeds from the coriander plant and used in many Indian dishes. Roasting and grinding them just before using is the best way to release their flavour. Ground coriander seeds are often mixed with ground cumin seeds to form *dhania-jeera* powder (coriander-cumin powder).

Cumin seeds (*jeera*): Aromatically spicy rather than hot; a spice used for many centuries. Its flavour is released when lightly roasted in a frying pan before using. The roasted seeds can be ground in a coffee grinder or a pestle and mortar and the powder stored in an airtight container. Often used to sprinkle over yogurt dishes, such as raitas, and chutneys.

Curry leaf (*kari patta*): The leaf of a tree native to India. When added to hot oil, curry leaves release a wonderful aroma. Used most often with vegetarian food, they are also used in fish and prawn (shrimp) curries. In southern India they are often combined with coconut. The dried leaves, which are available from Indian groceries, are a poor substitute. Fresh curry leaves can be stored for up to a week in a plastic bag in the fridge. Discard when brown marks appear on them.

Dill (fresh) (*soowa*): Aromatic and subtle, fresh dill adds a wonderful fragrance and flavour to many dishes, including rice, vegetable and meat preparations. It combines well with spinach and fenugreek when added to chicken. Only fresh dill should be used; the dried herb does not have the same flavour or aroma.

Edible silver leaf (*vark*): A delicate decoration, normally used to garnish desserts on special occasions. Can be bought in sheets from Indian groceries.

Fennel seeds (*sonf*): Lend meat and vegetables a slightly liquorice flavour. Most often used in India in *paan*, a mixture of seeds eaten after a meal to act as a mouth freshener and to aid digestion. (Please note: Betel-nut and *paan* chewing are factors directly associated with oral cancer. For more information, contact the British Dental

Association or the American Dental Association.)

Fenugreek leaves and seeds (*methi*): The seeds are used in many ready-made curry powders. Fenugreek leaves, freshly chopped, add a wonderful flavour to many meat dishes and are particularly delicious with potatoes. Only small quantities of the seeds should be used, as they have a slightly bitter flavour when used in excess.

Garam masala:
Garam means 'hot', and *masala* means 'spices'. Cardamom, cinnamon, cloves and bay leaves all form part of *garam masala*. Sometimes fennel seeds are also added. *Garam masala* adds both flavour and aroma. I favour using whole *garam masala* (cardamom pods, cinnamon sticks, bay leaves and whole cloves) for cooking, and use the powdered form to garnish dishes just before serving. Generally used with meat and rice, though rarely with fish

or vegetables, as the combination of powerful spices is considered too strong for delicate flavours.

Garlic (*lasan*): Popular the world over. One of the key flavours in a vast range of savoury Indian dishes. Puréed garlic can be kept in the fridge for several days,

Ginger (*adrak*): Derived from the root (rhizome) of the ginger plant and used for centuries as a flavouring and a medicinal cure-all. Puréed ginger can be kept in the fridge for several days, while fresh ginger will keep well for a couple of months.

Gram flour (*besan*): Made from hulled and split chickpeas (*chana daal*), and used to make pakoras (dumplings) and *bhajiyas* (deep-fried vegetable fritters). Acts as both a thickening and binding agent.

Green chillies (*hari mirch*): Available in a large range, they vary in the heat they generate! Fresh green chillies add

a wonderful flavour to many dishes. If the chillies aren't too hot you can leave the seeds in. If they are very hot, remove the seeds before using them or use them whole. They can be stored in a plastic bag in the fridge for up to a week. Fresh green chillies ground together with fresh coriander make a flavoursome paste, used as a base for sauces or marinades, known as *hara masala*.

Mint (*pudina*): A herb used as a flavouring since ancient times. Easy to grow, it adds a refreshing taste to curries and chutneys alike. Used in mint chutney (a must with most Indian meals) and biryanis (delicately flavoured rice with marinated meat). Should not be fried with spices, as it turns black quite quickly and changes the colour of the curry; add only at the end of cooking to retain its flavour.

Poppy seeds (*khus khus*): Mild and nutty flavoured; often ground to a paste with water to act as a thickening agent.

Seeds used to coat savoury items.

Saffron (*zafran*): A rare, precious and delicately flavoured spice. Historically, popular in societies with cultured aristocracies (who appreciated it) and a peasant class (who were able to provide the labour-intensive production it requires). The stigma of the crocus, it only blooms for a two-week period in the autumn and has to be picked by hand at dawn. A staggering 200,000-400,000 stigmas make only 1 kg of saffron. Used extensively in Mogul dishes, such as kormas (dishes cooked with rich spices) and pilaus.

Tamarind (*imli*): A very popular souring agent, the flesh is soaked in water and the juice squeezed out. Tamarind paste is now available from most Indian shops. Said to have a cooling effect on the system. Adds a refreshing flavour to dishes it is used in. Interestingly enough, it is one of the ingredients in Worcestershire sauce.

Turmeric (*haldi*): The root of a plant from the ginger family, which is cultivated in tropical countries. The root is boiled, peeled dried and ground. Retains its distinctive yellow colouring indefinitely but loses its flavour and aroma quickly, so should be bought in small quantities. Sometimes referred to as Indian saffron, though its spiciness is quite different to the delicate flavour of saffron.

The essential spice kitchen

Many people express a sense of intimidation with regard to what they imagine to be the great number of herbs and spices required for the preparation of Indian dishes. If the thought of collecting and storing vast quantities of spices deters you from experiencing the delights of Indian food, then rest assured: all you need to create a range of delicious, simple preparations are the following seven ingredients:

- Red chilli powder
- Turmeric
- Coriander-cumin powder
- Whole *garam masala* (cloves, cardamom pods, cinnamon sticks and bay leaves)
- Puréed ginger
- Puréed garlic (or crushed garlic cloves)
- Fresh coriander leaves

APPENDIX 5
Starters; Sweets and desserts; Utensils

STARTERS

In India, most meals aren't separated into courses, and so dishes that in the West would be classified as starters and main courses are served together. However, below I have listed a selection of dishes that could be offered under the heading of starters, to complement those listed in the starters chapter on page 35, with explanations as to what each one is.

Kachoris: Deep-fried pastries filled with vegetables or daals (lentils).

Mogo: Deep-fried cassava, often served as chips with chutney. An East African dish.

Papads (often referred to as poppadums):
Thin round Indian bread, often eaten with sweet pickles and *pudina* (mint) chutney while waiting for the main meal. In India, *papads* are often grilled over a direct flame, however in the West people tend to eat the deep-fried version.

Samosas: Ever-popular deep-fried pastry triangles stuffed with mince, chicken or vegetables.

SWEETS AND DESSERTS

Indians definitely have a sweet tooth. They need few excuses to indulge in their love for *mithai* (as sweet, sugary foods are known in India). These are distributed and offered to guests at every happy occasion, from an engagement to the passing of exams, and range from *barfis* and *ladoos*, which have a dry consistency, to *kheer*, and *ras malai*, which are semi-liquid. In the West, people often comment that, although they love eating an Indian meal, they find the desserts too sweet. I do not think the restaurants in the West do justice to the wonderful selection of Indian sweets. My favourite is *mishti doi* (sweet yogurt), a Bengali dessert. Unfortunately it is not generally available outside the state of Bengal, where it is sold in *mithai* shops, and for some unknown reason never tastes quite the same when I make it at home (hence the reason why you won't find a recipe for it here). I would recommend a visit to Calcutta if only to taste the wonderful sweet things – among them *mishti doi* – to be found there!

Barfi: Dry fudge-like sweet often flavoured with pistachio nuts, almonds, coconut, chocolate or carrots.

Falooda: Rich sweet milk drink, made from vermicelli and ice cream, and flavoured with rose syrup.

Gulab jamun: Milk-and-flour balls deep-fried and immersed in a rich syrup, often flavoured with nuts and saffron.

Jalebis: Pieces of orange-gold batter, deep-fried and served warm, soaked in a sweet syrup.

Ladoos: Sweet, round milk-and-gram-flour balls.

Mawa: Extraordinarily rich thickened milk, used in dessert-making.

Rasgulla: Milk-and-flour-sponge balls, served in a rich sugar syrup.

Ras malai: As above, but served in a creamy sauce.

Sandesh: A cottage-cheese and sugar-based fudge flavoured with lemon, orange, saffron or chocolate. A Bengali speciality.

Srikand: Popular Gujarati dessert made with concentrated yogurt flavoured with nuts and saffron.

UTENSILS
The following are all utensils typically used in an Indian kitchen.

Balti: Literally means 'bucket'! A wok-like pan.

Degchi: Pan with no handles.

Handi: Thick round-bottomed, wide-necked cooking pot.

Karai: Wok-like pan.

Katori: Small steel bowls, often served on a *thali* (see below), and used to keep different dishes separate. Particularly useful for runny daals (lentil dishes) and soupy curries.

Tandoor: Traditional Indian clay oven, which imparts a barbecue flavour to dishes. Also used to make bread.

Tapeli or *pateli:* Similar to a *degchi*.

Tawa: A slightly concave heavy-bottomed griddle pan made of cast iron. The nearest equivalent would be a flat heavy-bottomed frying pan. Originally used to make chapatis (flat bread), but now also used for a variety of curries.

Thali: Large steel platter on which *katoris* (see above) are served.

HINDI-ENGLISH GLOSSARY

achaars pickles

adrak ginger

ajowan carom seeds

amchoor mango powder

annar dana
pomegranate seeds

anda eggs

badam almond

baigan
aubergine (eggplant)

bajra millet

bandha gobi cabbage

besan gram flour

bhindi okra

cachumbar
raw vegetable relish

chaas buttermilk

chana daal
golden yellow lentils

chaval rice

daal dried lentils

dahi yogurt

dalchini cinnamon

dhania patta
coriander leaves

elaichi cardamom

gajjar carrot

ghee clarified butter

gur jaggery (molasses)

haldi turmeric

hari mirch green chillies

heeng asafoetida

imli tamarind

jaiphal nutmeg

javitri mace

jeera cumin seeds

kabuli chana chickpeas

kaju cashew nuts

kali mirch peppercorns

kalonji nigella

karela bitter gourd

kari patta curry leaf

kewda vetiver

khish mish raisins

khus khus poppy seeds

lal mirch red chilli

lasan garlic

lavang cloves

machi fish

malai cream

masoor daal red lentils

methi fenugreek

murg chicken

nariyal coconut

nimboo lime

paan betel leaves

panchporan Indian five-spice

paneer curd cheese

phool gobi cauliflower

pudina mint leaves

pyaz onion

rai mustard seeds

raita yogurt relish

sabut dhania
coriander seeds

shahjeera
black cumin seeds

sonf fennel seeds

soowa dill

suji semolina

tej patta bay leaf

til sesame seeds

toor daal deep yellow lentils

vark edible silver leaf

zafran saffron

BIBLIOGRAPHY

Hawkins, Kathryn and Duff, Gail, *A Dash of Spice*, London, The Reader's Digest Association Limited, Quarto Publishing plc, 1997

Panjabi, Camellia, *50 Great Curries of India*, London, Kyle Cathie Ltd, 1994

Rama Rau, Santa, and the editors of Time-Life Books, *The Cooking of India*, United States, Time Inc., 1969, revised 1972

Singh, Digvijaya, *Cooking Delights of the Maharajas: Exotic Dishes from the Princely Houses of Sailana*, 4th edn, Bombay, Vakils, Feffer & Simons Ltd, 1982

Svoboda, Robert E, *Ayurveda: Life, Health and Longevity*, London, Penguin Books Ltd, 1992

Westrip, Joyce P, *An ABC of Indian Food: From Aab Gosht to Zeera*, Devon, Prospect Books, 1996

STOCKISTS

While most supermarkets carry a limited range of Indian spices and ingredients, certain things, such as fresh curry leaves, big bunches of fresh coriander and certain types of lentils (daals) and flour (such as gram flour/*besan*) are only available from specialist shops. Here is a list of a few stockists of Indian ingredients and utensils in the UK and the USA.

UK STOCKISTS

Taj Stores, 112 Brick Lane, London E1, tel 020-7377 0061 Sells a range of vegetables, fruits and herbs, as well as all the spices and pulses needed to create an Indian meal.

Bangla Superstore, 17-19 Brick Lane, London E1, tel 020-7247 1009 General store selling all the usual ingredients, as well as halal meat (meat from animals killed according to Muslim law) and frozen fish.

London Oriental Foods, 122 Drummond Street, London NW1, tel 020-7387 3740 Stocks fresh vegetables, halal meat and many other ingredients.

VB & Sons, 147 Ealing Road, Wembley, tel 020-8795 0387 Sells a wide range of spices and ingredients, including pickles.

Bismillah Butchers, 141 Ealing Road, London, tel 020-8903 4922 For all halal meats (cut to order or pre-packed).

Giftos Cash & Carry, 115-119 The Broadway, Southall, tel 020-8574 8602

Dokal & Sons, 133-135 The Broadway, Southall, tel 020-8574 1647

Bhavins, 193 Upper Tooting Road, London SW17, tel 020-8672 7531 Stocks all the fresh fruit and vegetables as well as spices and other ingredients.

Jalpur Millers, 137 Harrison Road, Leicester, tel 0116-266 6206

Shiva Shakti Food,
4 & 6 Macdonald Road,
Leicester,
tel 0116-268 1622

Nisa Grocers, 131 Bridge
Road, Leicester,
tel 0116-276 6117

US STOCKISTS

Allworld Groceries,
344-B Maple Avenue
East, Vienna, VA 22180-
4716, tel 703-938 3400

Indian Spices, Gifts &
Appliances, 3901 Wilson
Boulevard, Arlington,
VA 22209-1921,
tel 703-522 0149/522
6900; fax 703-522 5232

Indo-Pak Spices,
422 Elden Street,
Herndon, VA 20170,
tel 703-709 5842;
fax 703-709 5144

Dana Bazaar,
1701 Rockville Pike,
Rockville, MD 20852-
1613, tel 301-231 7546

Indian Super Market,
8107 Fenton Street,
Silver Spring, MD 20910-
4757, tel 301-589 8417

Indus Foods & Halal
Meat, 15511 New

Hampshire Avenue,
Silver Spring, MD 20905-
4077, tel 301-989 9448

Anita Food Center,
21 Sherman Ave,
New York, NY,
tel 212-567 8200

India Bazaar, 69 1st Ave,
New York, NY,
tel 212-420 5906

Janata Spice Store,
85 1st Ave Fl. 1,
New York, NY,
tel 212-529 1815

Kalustyan Brothers,
123 Lexington Ave,
New York, NY,
tel 212-685 3451

Punjabi Grocery & Deli
Incorporated,
114 E 1st St, New York,
NY, tel 212-533 9048

Spice Corner,
135 Lexington Ave,
New York, NY,
tel 212-689 5182

Patel Brothers,
37-27 74th Street,
Jackson Heights, NY
11372, tel 718-898 3445

Bharat Bazaar, 11510
Washington Boulevard

(cross street is
Barryman), Culver City,
Los Angeles,
tel 310-398 6766
(for utensils as well
as spices)

India Sweet & Spices,
5992 W. Pico Boulevard
(corner of Pico and
Fairfax), Los Angeles,
tel 323-934 5193
(for utensils as well
as spices)

RECIPE INDEX

Hara masala (chilli and coriander paste) 31
Puréed ginger 32
Puréed garlic 32

STARTERS
Assorted *bhajiyas* (deep-fried vegetable fritters) 37
Sweet-corn *bhajiyas* (deep-fried sweet-corn fritters) 37
Onion *bhajiyas* (deep-fried onion fritters) 38
Papri chaat (*puris* topped with potatoes and chutney) 39
Tandoori cauliflower (marinated cauliflower with a chargrilled flavour) 39
Chicken *tikkas* (chicken pieces marinated in yogurt and spices) 40
Chicken *malai* kebabs (creamy chicken kebabs) 41
Aloo chaap (seasoned mincemeat encased in mashed potato) 42
Aloo vadas (spicy potato balls in batter) 42
Shami kebabs (stuffed lentil kebabs) 43
Seekh kebabs (long kebabs) 44
Reshmi kebabs (delicate chicken kebabs) 45
Meat cutlets (hamburgers with a difference) 45
Vegetable cutlets 46
Dahi vadas (lentil donuts with yogurt and chutney) 47
Aloo tikkis (potato patties stuffed with peas and spices) 47
Paneer tikkas (curd cheese morsels) 48
Smoked salmon *tikkas* (smoked salmon morsels) 49

VEGETABLES AND VEGETARIAN
Masala wale aloo (spicy Bombay potatoes) 53
Tilwale aloo (potatoes with sesame seeds) 53

Gujarati-style potatoes (potatoes with a hint of lemon and sugar) 54

Sag aloo (spinach with potatoes) 55

Aloo gobi (potatoes with cauliflower) 56

Aloo, mattar aur tamatar (potatoes, peas and tomatoes) 56

Quick spicy sweet corn 57

Quick green beans 58

Quick mixed vegetables 58

Mushroom *do pyaza* (mushrooms with onions) 59

Chana batata (chickpeas and potatoes) 60

Sookha gobi (cauliflower with ginger and cumin) 61

Tarka daal (lentils infused with garlic) 61

Mattar paneer (peas with curd cheese) 62

Bhindi ki bhaji (okra with onions) 63

Nariyal wala bhutta (sweet corn in coconut) 63

Anda ka kheema (spicy scrambled eggs) 64

Vegetable *makhanwala* (vegetables in a creamy sauce) 73

Punjabi *chana* (Punjabi-style chickpeas) 73

Stuffed green peppers 74

Bagara baigan (spicy sautéed aubergine) 75

Dahi ki curry (yogurt curry) 76

Pakoras (gram-flour dumplings) 76

MEAT

A basic curry sauce 81

Kheema par anda (savoury mince with baked eggs) 81

Sag gosht (spicy meat with spinach) 82

Rogan josh (spicy red lamb cooked with yogurt and saffron) 83

Kheema mattar (mince with peas) 84

Chaap (mince with chilli and coriander paste and lemon juice) 85

Gosht-e-Mehboob (tender pieces of lamb in a rich, robust sauce) 85

Tawa gosht (succulent leg of lamb cooked with spices in a tawa) 86

Lamb *pasanda* (lamb in a mild, creamy sauce with almonds) 87

Methi gosht (spicy meat with fenugreek) 88

Aab gosht (a classic, delicately flavoured lamb dish) 89

Achaar gosht (lamb with pickle spices) 90

Daal *gosht* (spicy lentils with lamb) 91

Nariyal wala gosht (lamb with coconut milk and fresh coriander) 92

CHICKEN

Murgi ka salna (simple, everyday chicken curry) 95

Chicken *tikka masala* (marinated smoked chicken in a rich, creamy sauce) 95

Zafrani murg (chicken with saffron) 96

Murg dilkhush (chicken with coconut milk, potatoes and saffron) 97

Jeera chicken (chicken with cumin) 98

Chicken korma (chicken in a mild, creamy sauce) 98

Karai chicken (1) (chicken cooked in a *karai* with peppers and tomatoes) 99

Karai chicken (2) 100

Dhania chicken (coriander chicken) 101

Chicken *jalfrezi* (spicy chicken with peppers and onions) 101

Chicken *do pyaza* (spicy chicken with onions) 102

Kuku paka (chicken with a sauce of creamy coconut, fresh coriander and lemon juice) 103

Balti chicken (chicken with almonds, fenugreek and cream) 104

Chicken Madras (hot, fiery, spicy chicken) 105

Chicken with green peppers 106

FISH AND SEAFOOD

Fried fish with potatoes 109

Machi ka salna (spicy fish curry) 109

Prawn *patia* (sweet and sour prawn curry) 110

Masala prawns and potatoes (spicy prawns and potatoes) 111

Amritsari fish (fried fish) 112

RICE

Pilau rice 116

Dill pilau 116

Vegetable pilau 117

Brown rice 117

Jeera pilau (cumin pilau) 118

Fish pilau 119

Gosht pilau (*akni* – lamb and potato pilau) 120

Masoor pilau (rice, mince and lentil pilau) 121

Bhuni khichri (rice and lentil pilau) 122

Chicken *tikka* biryani (delicately flavoured rice with marinated chicken pieces) 123

Lamb *pathani* biryani (rice with lamb, spinach, fenugreek and sweet corn) 124

BREAD

Chapatis 129

Puris 129

Parathas 130

Aloo parathas (*parathas* stuffed with potatoes) 130

Naan 131

ACCOMPANIMENTS

Pudina chutney (mint chutney) 135

Quick mint sauce 135

Mitha chutney (date and tamarind chutney) 135

Nariyal ka chutney (coconut and coriander chutney) 136

Onion and tomato cachumbar 137

Cucumber and onion cachumbar 137

Kheera ka raita (cucumber raita) 138

Aloo ka raita (potato raita) 138

DESSERTS

Shahi tukra (rich, creamy bread pudding with saffron and cardamom) 141

Pineapple *halwa* (pineapple, cream and saffron pudding) 141

Carrot *halwa* (carrot, cream and saffron pudding) 142

Seerkhurma (rich milk drink) 143

Kulfi (Indian ice cream) 143

Mango mousse 144

Kheer (Indian rice pudding) 145

Firni (rice pudding with a difference!) 145

Lassi (refreshing sweet or savoury yogurt drink) 146

RECIPE A-Z

A basic curry sauce **81**

Aab gosht **89**

Achaar gosht **90**

Aloo chaap **42**

Aloo gobi **56**

Aloo ka raita **138**

Aloo parathas **130**

Aloo tikkis **47**

Aloo vadas **42**

Aloo, mattar aur tamatar **56**

Amritsari fish **112**

Anda ka kheema **64**

Assorted *bhajiyas* **37**

Bagara baigan **75**

Balti chicken **104**

Bhindi ki bhaji **63**

Bhuni khichri **122**

Brown rice **117**

Carrot *halwa* **142**

Chaap **85**

Chana batata **60**

Chapatis **129**

Chicken *do pyaza* **102**

Chicken *jalfrezi* **101**

Chicken *korma* **98**

Chicken Madras **105**

Chicken *malai* kebabs **41**

Chicken *tikka* biryani **123**

Chicken *tikka* masala **95**

Chicken *tikkas* **40**

Chicken with green peppers **106**

Cucumber and onion *cachumbar* **137**

Daal *gosht* **91**

Dahi ki curry **76**

Dahi vadas **47**

Dhania chicken **101**

Dill pilau **116**

Firni **145**

Fish pilau **119**

Fried fish with potatoes **109**

Gosht pilau **120**

Gosht-e-Mehboob **85**

Gujarati-style potatoes **54**

Hara masala **31**

Jeera chicken **98**

Jeera pilau **118**

Karai chicken (1) **99**

Karai chicken (2) **100**

Kheema mattar **84**

Kheema par anda **81**

Kheer **145**

Kheera ka raita **138**

Kuku paka **103**

Kulfi **143**

Lamb *pasanda* **87**

Lamb *pathani* biryani **124**

Lassi **146**

Machi ka salna **109**

Mango mousse **144**

Masala prawns and potatoes **111**

Masala wale aloo **53**

Masoor pilau **121**

Mattar paneer **62**

Meat cutlets **45**

Methi gosht **88**

Mitha chutney **135**

Murg dilkhush **97**

Murgi ka salna **95**

Mushroom *do pyaza* **59**

Naan **131**

Nariyal ka chutney **136**

Nariyal wala bhutta **63**

Nariyal wala gosht **92**

Onion and tomato *cachumbar* **137**

Onion *bhajiyas* **38**

Pakoras **76**

Paneer tikkas **48**

Papri chaat   **39**

Parathas   **130**

Pilau rice   **116**

Pineapple *halwa*   **141**

Prawn *patia*   **110**

Pudina chutney   **135**

Punjabi *chana*   **73**

Puréed garlic   **32**

Puréed ginger   **32**

Puris   **129**

Quick green beans   **58**

Quick mint sauce   **135**

Quick mixed
vegetables   **58**

Quick spicy sweet
corn   **57**

Reshmi kebabs   **45**

Rogan josh   **83**

Sag aloo   **55**

Sag gosht   **82**

Seekh kebabs   **44**

Seerkhurma   **143**

Shahi tukra   **141**

Shami kebabs   **43**

Smoked salmon
tikkas   **49**

Sookha gobi   **61**

Stuffed green peppers   **74**

Sweet-corn *bhajiyas*   **37**

Tandoori cauliflower   **39**

Tarka daal   **61**

Tawa gosht   **86**

Tilwale aloo   **53**

Vegetable cutlets   **46**

Vegetable
makhanwala   **73**

Vegetable pilau   **117**

*Zafrani mur*g   **96**